A Zero-Based Look at
Zero-Base Budgeting

A Zero-Based Look at Zero-Base Budgeting

Why Its Failures in State Government are Being Duplicated in Washington

Thomas H. Hammond
and
Jack H. Knott

Transaction Books
New Brunswick (U.S.A.) and London (U.K.)

Copyright © 1980 by Transaction, Inc.
New Brunswick, New Jersey 08903

All rights reserved under International and Pan-American Copyright
Conventions. No part of this book may be reproduced or transmitted
in any form or by any means, electronic or mechanical, including pho-
tocopy, recording, or any information storage and retrieval system,
without prior permission in writing from the publisher. All inquiries
should be addressed to Transaction Books, Rutgers—The State University, New Brunswick, New Jersey 08903.

Library of Congress Catalog Number: 79-65228
ISBN: 0-87855-365-7 (cloth)
Printed in the United States of America

Library of Congress Cataloging in Publication Data

Hammond, Thomas H   1947-
    A zero-based look at zero-base budgeting.

    Bibliography: p.
    Includes index.
    1. Zero-base budgeting—United States. I. Knott,
Jack H., joint author. II. Title.
HJ2052.H35   353.007'22   79-65228
ISBN 0-87855-365-7

To
Jane M. Fraser
and
Vicki Bergsma Knott

Contents

Preface

Zero-base budgeting (ZBB) is the most popular budget reform of the decade. Several state and local governments have adopted it, as have over a hundred private corporations. When Jimmy Carter became governor of Georgia in 1971, he introduced ZBB into Georgia administration. Following his election to the presidency, ZBB became the standard method of budgeting for the federal government.

Numerous articles have been written about zero-base budgeting. Most of them acclaim its ability to reduce bureaucratic waste, eliminate administrative duplication and overlap, and improve governmental effectiveness. Several books describe in great detail how to implement a ZBB system.

What is lacking in this extensive literature is a careful and thorough assessment of how well ZBB has actually worked in the many places where it has been tried. Nor is there any substantial critique of ZBB from the perspective of what is known about politics and public management. Our purpose in writing this book is to address these two issues.

When we began our work in the summer of 1977, the most pressing question on our minds was: how will ZBB fare in the federal government? To answer this question we first needed to find out whether ZBB's claims had been substantiated in the places that had already tried it. The evidence came from several articles and manuscripts written about state and city ZBB efforts. Although these pieces were invaluable to us, their authors were seldom concerned with the significance of ZBB for the federal government or with the broader implications of their findings for politics and budgeting. Nevertheless, a consistent pattern did emerge from these case studies. What budgeters did with ZBB in Georgia was quite similar to what their colleagues did with it in Texas, New Jersey, and elsewhere, and in no place did it produce what was hoped for.

We were able to draw generalizations from these case studies, but did they apply to the federal government as well? It might be argued that state and local budgeting is quite different from federal budgeting. The federal government has greater analytical resources, for instance, and more funding leeway. Perhaps these circumstances make our assessment not entirely applicable to federal budgeting. It might also be argued that, since the federal effort is so new, we should not prejudge it; times have changed since earlier budget reform efforts, and maybe people have learned from past mistakes. But while evidence on the federal ZBB effort is still limited, what there is substantiates in great measure our analysis of the state and local ZBB experiences.

One additional way we have tried to overcome the limitations of the case studies is by relating our findings to what is known about organizations, politics and budgeting. Budgeting is one of the few areas in public administration in which there is a body of knowledge and theory useful enough to apply to the real world. ZBB shares a certain logic with past budget reforms (such as PPBS and Performance Budgeting), and some of its procedures are quite similar to other management techniques (such as Management-by-Objectives). Studies of these earlier efforts have been done that are rich both in theory and in data. We have been able to draw on this organizational and political literature as a way of evaluating the fragmentary data on the current ZBB efforts.

Our analysis, then, is more than a simple assessment of a particular budget technique. Rather, it links ZBB to some broader issues in politics and public administration. With ZBB's similarity to other reform and management techniques, the experiences with ZBB can teach us what will and will not work in budget reform.

The origins of this book go back to the seminar on budgeting and politics that Aaron Wildavsky used to teach at the University of California, Berkeley. Our intellectual debt to him is obvious and much appreciated. Oftentimes we thought we were making an original observation, only to discover he had said it better fifteen years ago. Aaron encouraged us to undertake this project, and we thank him for his continued support during the ups and downs of its completion. Nelson Polsby also played a hand in launching the project: he left for London on a Guggenheim Fellowship in Summer 1977 soon after encouraging us to proceed with our plans to put together a reader on ZBB; when he returned the "reader" was defunct, and the "introductory essay" for it had grown into a book of its own.

Jane Fraser helped us in many ways. Her knowledge of economics and operations research proved invaluable in clarifying certain arguments and in fitting various analytical bits and pieces together. In particular, she aided us in making our arguments about ZBB's ranking procedures. Without her advice, these parts would have suffered considerably. She, Jonathan Bendor, and David Leonard commented on several drafts of the manuscript. Jon was especially helpful in relating the findings from the case studies to relevant political and organizational theories. David made a number of useful comments, and in particular prodded us to give greater attention to the question of whether ZBB was a better kind of incremental budgeting. Irv Lefberg read a draft of our Conclusion, and alerted us to some relevant literature in a variety of fields, including judicial decision making. Robin Lefberg produced the final form of the illustrations.

For all this assistance, we are grateful. One of the most enjoyable aspects of writing something like this was that it gave us an excuse to talk with some stimulating people. None of them has yet disclaimed responsibility for how we have used his or her ideas, though we are happy to absolve them of responsibility should they so desire.

Several institutions supported the research and writing of this manuscript. The Graduate School of Public Policy at U.C. Berkeley generously supplied secretarial support and also distributed an earlier version of the manuscript as Working Paper Number 82. We thank the competent and helpful librarians of Berkeley's Institute of Governmental Studies who aided us in our use of its holdings on state and local government. Finally, we gratefully acknowledge the aid to our efforts given by the UNIX and INTERCOM computer text-editing facilities maintained by the Computer Centers of the University of California, Berkeley and the University of Washington, and the Departments of Political Science there which both provided ample computer funds. Rik Littlefield of the U.W. Computer Center provided indispensable assistance in transferring the manuscript from Berkeley's UNIX system to UW's INTERCOM system. Ric Johnston of the U.W. Department of Political Science and the Center for Quantitative Studies ably solved many additional problems. A pair of more genial, patient, and astute tutors would be impossible to find. Tom Hammond used the text-editing programs to do most of the initial typing, editing, and retyping of countless versions of the manuscript. The time and effort saved by these wonders of modern technology was enormous; cutting-and-pasting has given way to electronics.

Our book could not have been possible without the earlier work by participants in and observers of various federal, state, and local ZBB efforts. We especially want to thank George S. Minmier for granting us permission to use material from his work, *An Evaluation of the Zero-Base Budgeting System in Governmental Institutions* (Atlanta,

Georgia: School of Business Administration, Georgia State University, 1975). His study of Georgia is by far the most thorough and useful investigation to date of any ZBB effort. Without his careful and even-handed research, our own study would barely have been possible.

Thomas H. Hammond
Jack H. Knott

Chapter 1

Introduction

Another wave of budget reform is sweeping through the federal government. This decade's event is called zero-base-budgeting—ZBB for short. Like its predecessors, ZBB is supposed to make government more effective and efficient. Priorities among government programs are to be established. Duplication and overlap are to be spotlighted and eliminated. Resources are to be reallocated from inefficient or outmoded programs to more worthy ones.

Like the Planning-Programming-Budgeting Systems (PPBS) of the 1960s, ZBB aspires to a comprehensive examination of government expenditures. But unlike PPBS, ZBB had extensive testing in state and city governments before adoption by the federal government. Surprisingly, however, these early experiences show ZBB to have had little impact on either budgets or budgeting. This was true even in President Carter's home state of Georgia, where as governor he first introduced ZBB to government budgeting.

Our purpose in this book is to answer the questions which naturally arise: Why has ZBB failed where it has been tried?; and, Can we expect it to work any better in Washington, when it has failed everywhere else?

In answering the first question, we will examine ZBB at work in the state and city government. Various claims have been made for ZBB by its proponents; discounting for the inevitable hyperbole, do these claims hold up? Are priorities established? Does ZBB save money or lead to the discovery of wasteful and inefficient programs? Does it allocate resources in a demonstrably better way?

Our judgment is that, when all is said and done, little is changed. Few resources are reallocated due to ZBB, and few decisions are made differently. And in the process of following ZBB's complex procedures, officials spend a huge amount of time, energy, and money which could be used more fruitfully elsewhere.

1

Since these procedures appear to be quite "rational" in character, at least in the abstract, and yet they fail to produce the desired results, we also take a detailed look at the procedures themselves. ZBB requires budgeters to clarify objectives, measure performance, consider alternatives, rank activities in order of priority, and choose only the most important. But it turns out that these procedures are less "rational," even on their own terms, than first impressions suggest. No less importantly, they fail to address the main problems of government budgeting. Under some conditions, in fact, ZBB may even lead to clearly erroneous decisions.

Evidence from the state and city governments also indicates that ZBB's procedures have required extensive modification to make them workable at all. A close reading of the writings of ZBB's creator, Peter A. Pyhrr, a management consultant and former advisor to Governor Carter in Georgia, shows that Pyhrr himself has proposed extensive changes in the original procedures, with the same goal of workability in mind. Do these modified procedures improve budgeting? Our conclusion is that they do not, although they do convert ZBB into that which it is trying to replace, namely, traditional incremental budgeting.

Given these numerous problems, we also try to come to grips with the question of why chief executives persist in adopting ZBB, and, for that matter, why users down in the bureaucracies sometimes also seem to like ZBB. We advance a number of plausible reasons for this paradoxical behavior and these unexpected attitudes, but these will only be inferences. No scholar has yet dealt adequately with these problems, nor will we try to do so here.

All this is not to say that Jimmy Carter will have no impact on the federal budget. From his first year in office alone one can point to a large number of actions which President Ford would neither have taken nor proposed, and many of which have important budgetary consequences. Many of these actions we applaud. But the point is that ZBB has had little to do with these decisions. It is Jimmy Carter who is making these decisions, and not Gerald Ford, and that is what makes all the difference. Jimmy Carter's appointees also differ from their Ford Administration predecessors, but again, their decisions are different because of who they are, what they want to do, and who their constituencies are, and not because of ZBB. Whatever effect ZBB is likely to have on budgets and budgeting in the Carter Administration will be negligible in comparison to these other factors.

Our analysis proceeds in the following manner. In Chapters 2 and 3 we describe and analyze how ZBB is supposed to work and how it does work. We discuss the role of activities and objectives, the formulation of decision packages, the use of performance measures, the creation of minimums and alternatives, the process of ranking, and the use of cutoff lines. (These terms will soon become familiar to the uninitiated.) The problems that result and the political strategies that evolve are described. Chapter 4 is an overall evaluation of ZBB in practice; that is, does it accomplish for budgeters what its proponents say it does? Because for the most part the claims are unsupported by the evidence and yet many participants in the process retain positive feelings towards ZBB, we also consider the unanticipated "benefits" of ZBB which may account for this odd situation.

In Chapter 5, we place zero-base budgeting in a broader context. After discussing problems with the kind of rationality that it exemplifies, we present another kind of rationality that may be more appropriate for government budgeting. We next consider the possibility that although ZBB works in practice as incremental budgeting, it might in fact be a *better kind* of incrementalism. Finally, we consider whether there are ways of getting some of the benefits that ZBB is supposed to bring, without bearing the costs that ZBB entails.

Before proceeding with our analysis, it will be helpful to describe in some detail exactly how ZBB procedures are supposed to work. It must be stressed at the outset, however, that no one standard set of procedures exists. Different organizations have applied ZBB in different ways.[1]

Zero-base budgeting begins with the identification of the organizational *decision units* which are to prepare the first parts of the budget. No hard-and-fast rule exists to determine where these units are to be located or how large they are supposed to be. Generally, however, if a government organization has detailed budget units or a private business has established cost centers, the decision units are to correspond to them. It is recommended, for example, that a decision unit be specified at the level of a single budget account in an existing organizational subunit.[2] In an organization with a well-developed program budget, the decision units may reflect the lowest-level program elements if there are separate organizational units within the program element. However, ZBB inventor Pyhrr indicates that decision units may also be "major capital projects, special work assignments, or major projects."[3] The choice of decision units is thus based mostly on traditional budget practices and existing organizational structures.

But other factors do enter into the choice of decision units. The most important is the identification of governmental objectives. The Office of Management and Budget's ZBB guidelines, for example, emphasize the clarifying of objectives, along with the determination of decision units, as the two starting points in the ZBB process.[4] Just how the choice of objectives is supposed to influence the choice of decision units is, however, not clearly spelled out and appears to be left up to the individual departments, a fact which we will examine in more detail later in the analysis.

Following the identification of the organization's decision units, the next step is for these decision units to draw up what are called *decision packages*. These packages form the building blocks for the rest of the ZBB procedures. A decision package is a document that provides justification for and a description of the various activities and programs of a decision unit. (Each decision unit will draw up several decision packages.) Although the format for decision packages varies somewhat, each package basically provides the following kinds of information:[5]

1. A statement of the objectives of the program.
2. A description of the activities in the program.
3. A listing of the benefits and costs of the program.
4. Workload and performance measures.
5. Alternative ways of accomplishing the objectives.

In order to avoid excessive paperwork and time, this information is usually condensed onto a two-page form.

Formulating a decision package requires as a first step that a decision unit determine appropriate *objectives* for each program. There are many different mutually exclusive ways of achieving an objective, however. Such *alternative activities* must also be identified and the best of them chosen on the basis of its ability to achieve the objective. Once this choice is made, several different levels of effort (in dollars, usually) for this activity are laid out, and a *minimum level of effort* is identified. This minimum level is usually considered to be that level below which spending any money on the activity is useless or wasteful. A minimum level of effort of a given activity is summarized in the *minimum level of effort decision package*, or simply a "minimum."

With this minimum-level-of-effort package in hand, incremental funding levels above the minimum are then identified. Each increment to the minimum is also described in a decision package. As these *incremental packages* are added sequentially to the minimum package, proposed spending on a given activity approaches and then exceeds the current level of effort of the activity. (What constitutes the "minimum" and how big the increments are vary from organization to organization.) These decision packages together constitute the total budget request for a given decision unit. Each unit that prepares decision packages will normally be engaged in a variety of activities, and the unit will thus prepare several minimum level packages (one for each activity), along with several incremental packages for each activity.

To illustrate how decision package information is displayed, it is helpful to look at some sample decision packages from the OMB guidelines. The examples are from the Mental Health Administration in the Department of Health, Education, and Welfare. The specific activity that is described is the program of federal support of Community Mental Health Centers. (CMHC). In the first decision package (1 out of 4) the recommendation is to fund the CMHC at $120,000,000, which is less than the current effort; package 2 considers adding $20,000,000, bringing the program up to the current level of funding of $140,000,000. Package 3 proposes adding $10,000,000, for a total outlay of $150,000,000; and Package 4 lays out a plan for spending another $10,000,000 for a cumulative total request of $160,000,000. In each decision package the impact of the specific proposal on both the short and long-term objectives of the program is estimated. Information also is provided on the cost of each proposal, along with a time schedule for achieving the objectives.

The kinds of activities that constitute a decision package vary considerably. In the OMB illustration, the subject of the package is a federal grant to local communities. Other activities which can be described in decision packages range from the measurement of urban air pollution samples to the components of the Space Shuttle project in NASA. No one rule covers all possible cases of what should be in a decision package; in his book Pyhrr states that the subjects of decision packages can be people, projects, capital expenditures, services, or even line-item budget expenditures.[6] Although the clarification of objectives is supposed to affect the dividing up of activities and programs into decision packages, just how this is supposed to be done remains unclear. All that is prescribed is that decision unit managers are to decide what activities are appropriate in consultation with higher authorities.

Once the decision packages are formulated, the responsible manager or official must then *rank in order of priority* all the decision packages, producing one list with the decision packages in order of priority. High priority decision packages rank at the top, low priority packages at the bottom. Minimum level packages must always be ranked higher than their associated increments, but an increment to one minimum level package may be ranked higher than a minimum level package of another activity.

These rankings are then submitted to a higher authority. This person (or group, in some cases) will be receiving rankings from several subordinates. The task at this stage is to *consolidate* these separate rankings into *one* ranking based on the judgments of the official or group at this position in the organization. Their judgments are to be based on the cost/benefit and performance measures displayed in the decision packages. This procedure is repeated on up the hierarchy of the organization. Ultimately, there is produced one consolidated ranking for the entire organization. At this top level, a separate judgment is made as to how much money is to be spent. The "costs" of each decision package are then simply added up in sequence, starting with the highest priority items in the ranking and moving on down the list. When the total accumulated cost reaches the amount that is to be spent, a *cutoff line* is imposed. All decision packages above the cutoff line will be funded; all packages below the line will not.

In sum, ZBB procedures involve five basic steps:

1. The identification of organizational entities, referred to as decision units, for which budgets are to be prepared.
2. The clarification of the objectives of decision units' programs.
3. The drawing up of standard documents, called decision packages, which provide a justification for and a description of the decision units' programs and activities.
4. The ranking of these decision packages in order of priority.
5. The consolidation of these decision package rankings for review and final decision by a higher authority.

These are the procedures of zero-base budgeting. The question is, do they work?

Notes

1. The following description is based on a careful reading of the writings of ZBB proponents who have prescribed how the procedures are supposed to work. Nevertheless, there are ambiguities in the process. Because there has not yet been a thorough analysis of how these procedures are carried out in practice, our description inevitably reflects the limitations of these original sources.
2. Donald F. Haider, "Zero-Base: Federal Style," *Public Administration Review* 37 (July/August 1977), pp. 400-407.

3. Peter Pyhrr, "The Zero-Base Approach To Government Budgeting," *Public Administration Review* 37 (January/February 1977), p. 3.
4. Office of Management and Budget Bulletin 77-9, *The Federal Register*, Monday, May 2, 1977, Part VII, pp. 22342-56.
5. From Peter A. Pyhrr, *Zero-Base Budgeting: A Practical Management Tool For Evaluating Expenses* (New York: John Wiley & Sons, 1973), p. 6; see also Pyhrr, "The Zero-Base Approach to Government Budgeting," p. 3.
6. Pyhrr, *Zero-Base Budgeting*, p. 51.

Chapter 2

A Political Analysis of
ZBB's Procedures

A first reaction to ZBB's procedures is how "rational" they seem. What could be wrong with specifying objectives, grouping activities together, setting priorities on programs, and then funding only the most important? If we were to *define* rationality in budgeting, we would come up with something like these procedures. Indeed, it might be said that such procedures *embody* the concept of rationality in government.[1]

Unfortunately, the same could be said about the previous budget reforms. They also appeared to embody rationality. A cursory examination of "performance budgeting" in the 1950s, "program budgeting" (PPBS) in the 1960s, and "Management by Objectives" in the late 1960s and early 1970s will show that they all share ZBB's logical structure. What these reforms also share is the fact that they were all failures.[2] They didn't do what was hoped, and they were all abandoned. Can we find out why procedures that look so good always seem to fail? In order to understand why, let us subject ZBB's procedures to a careful examination.

Zero-base budgeting begins with the injunction, "First of all, define your objectives." The OMB zero-base budgeting guidelines in 1977, for example, state that the main purpose of ZBB is to "[e]stablish, for all managerial levels in an agency, objectives against which accomplishments can be identified and measured . . ." One benefit of ZBB is the focusing of the budget process "on a comprehensive analysis of objectives..."[3]

What could be more rational than to clarify our goals in order to know what to do? In simply clarifying our goals, however, we confront three important problems. One is that clarifying goals sometimes defeats our purposes in doing so. A second is that clarifying goals is different from agreeing on goals. A third is that it is harder than we

9

might think to define our goals; this means that we may overestimate how accurately they reflect our intentions when we do define them.[4]

To clarify our goals in politics may be to lose political support. A dovish Eugene McCarthy won a considerable amount of hawkish support in the 1968 New Hampshire primary against President Lyndon Johnson simply because he was seen as an alternative to an unpopular incumbent. A more recent example is Jimmy Carter's 1976 presidential campaign. According to reporters who followed him during the campaign, he had both a predilection and a talent for pleasant-sounding ambiguity; more clarity on his part may have meant fewer votes.[5]

What is true in electoral politics may often be true in legislative politics. A good way of tying up legislation would be to require legislators to agree as to what exactly the objectives of a bill are, and what their motives are in supporting it.[6] Our personal lives are little different. To teach a child "tact" is to teach him how to conceal his true thoughts and feelings in the interests of social harmony. And would anyone ever marry if a man and a woman had to agree on the precise objectives of marriage?

Political support is also necessary for the success of government programs. Support from broad segments of the public, from interest groups, from legislators, from party leaders, and from bureaucrats is essential. To clarify the precise purposes of government programs may be to alienate one or more of these key actors. This is not inevitably the case, but it is probably the case often enough to make us think twice about willy-nilly clarification.

What if we do proceed to define and clarify our goals? We will find, first, that we have very many goals. An attempt at implementing Management by Objectives in HEW in the early 1970s produced some 1870 "goals" in HEW alone. At the Departmental level, seventy goals were identified; the six agency heads and ten regional directors produced an additional 300 somewhat narrower objectives; and the bureaus that make up the six agencies produced another 1500 still more specific and narrow objectives.[7] Of course, this massive list left out organizational goals (increased budgets, bureaucratic prestige, and so forth) and all the personal goals that executives and bureaucrats might have. After defining even only the "public" ones, we may also find them contradictory and incompatible with each other. This does not mean that some of them are the "right" goals, and the others "wrong."

Consider United States foreign policy in the Middle East as an illustration of conflicting and competing policy goals. Among our objectives are a permanent peace settlement, an uninterrupted supply of OPEC oil, a viable and defendable Israeli state, and only minor Soviet influence in the region. In addition, we desire to maintain a favorable balance of trade for the United States. Few people are against any one of these goals in principle, but in practice they conflict with each other. Selling arms to both sides jeopardizes peace, although it does aid our trade balance; supporting Israel threatens uninterrupted oil supplies, but it does defend the lone democratic state in the region; selling arms to OPEC countries threatens Israel, even though it expands our influence in the Arab world. In short, the objectives of our Mideast policy are contradictory. Yet we are not willing to give up any one of them. And although the Mideast is a particularly difficult policy area, multiple and incompatible objectives also characterize our policies toward many other areas, such as Greece and Turkey, Japan, Korea and China, and Eastern Europe.

Are multiple and conflicting objectives the preserve of foreign policy? Hardly. A case in point is the federal government's policy toward the automotive industry. Congress has required car manufacturers to build safety features into new models, lower fuel consumption, and tighten emission standards. But with today's technology, not all of these goals are achievable at once. The goals work against each other. Heavier cars are safer cars, but at the cost of fuel consumption. Should government choose among these goals? It is hard to know which goal to abandon. Some 40,000 people are killed in auto accidents every year, and hundreds of thousands are injured. Smog and other air pollutants contribute significantly to lung diseases and a variety of other ailments. Consumption of gasoline by automobiles is a key contributor to the nation's energy problems. Clarifying our goals here does little to solve our problems. All it does is point out to participants in the debate that their goals are to some extent incompatible. This they no doubt already know.

Less tangible goals may also be incompatible. The Bakke "reverse discrimination" case placed the Supreme Court in the unenviable position of choosing between the time-honored objective of basing entrance to higher education on merit and the pressing purpose of helping minorities obtain high quality education. But since many Americans are unwilling to make university entrance open to all, however unqualified, nor are many others agreeable to dispensing with affirmative action, the Court found itself torn between two widely respected principles. As a result, the divided Court downplayed the implications of the case by basing its decision on the 1964 Civil Rights Act instead of the 14th Amendment's "equal protection" clause, thereby allowing the government to continue to pursue both goals at once: Mr. Bakke could go to medical school, but affirmative action programs were still legal.

Similarly, an important concern such as governmental "efficiency" in water resource projects may conflict with our conception of an "equitable" outcome. To build an efficient dam—one with a high benefit to cost ratio—does not mean that it is wise to build the dam or that the distribution of benefits from it is to our liking. But doing something that is beneficial to the groups we support—almost any government expenditure is beneficial to somebody somewhere—does not mean that it is being efficiently done.

Organizations are also concerned about very intangible resources, such as reputation for wisdom, judgment, and trustworthiness, that make it possible to achieve their more concrete objectives. To pursue some tangible objective, like building a dam, without simultaneous attention to the intangible matters may, at least in the long run, make attainment of the tangible objectives more difficult. Even the most public-minded of civil servants must look out for the interests and reputation of his organization. If he doesn't, who will? No one wants a Transportation Department that is not an effective advocate of transportation needs.

If we are going to require that objectives be defined and clarified, our task is made vastly more difficult if we also require that the objectives be agreed upon. If ZBB's proponents want to take the politics out of budgeting, there is little that will cause a *greater increase* in political activity than requiring agreement on objectives. People have conflicting objectives. When they are nonetheless able to agree on what government programs to pursue, it is not necessarily a sign that agreement on objectives has been reached. Fast growing tax revenues, for instance, may make it likely that there are enough resources available to "buy off," so to speak, each participant. Spreading budget growth among several agencies can do wonders for reaching agreement on which government programs to support, even if it does not produce consensus on what the programs are supposed to accomplish. Organizational theorists have come to call such available but uncommitted resources "slack."[8] When there is plenty of slack, other things being equal, overt conflict is low. As slack declines, conflict increases. When the economy is going badly and a firm's profits decline, or when an agency's budget must be cut, people find themselves forced out of necessity to make the difficult choice among competing goals. Otherwise, the organization itself may not survive.

But when things are going satisfactorily, that is, when there is sufficient slack, agreeing on the means and getting on with the job may be preferable to endless haggling over what the ends are to be.[9] In many cases, the opportunity costs of requiring definition and agreement on goals outweighs the policy benefits (if any) of such clarification.

If we *do* nonetheless require people to agree on their objectives before they act jointly, what they normally produce are vague generalities, after fighting about—and not agreeing on—specifics: "national security," "community development," "racial justice," "a clean environment," and so forth. Even Peter Drucker, the popularizer of Management by Objectives, has confessed that his earlier views concerning forcing agreement on objectives were erroneous:

> It was very clear then that the purpose of asking the question—'what are our objectives'—was to get unanimity. For thirty years, I not only believed it, I preached it, and occasionally I tried to practice it. I was wrong. If you try to get unanimity, you'll paper over the cracks, and you inhibit understanding. The purpose is to bring out divergent views.[10]

But despite Drucker's apostasy, his early views on forcing agreement on objectives remain firmly entrenched in American managerial ideology.[11]

Does Drucker's newly stated purpose for MBO—to bring out divergent views—give us cause to do what he now says? One purpose of clarifying objectives is to improve accountability. If an agency clearly states what its purposes are, then it is easier for evaluators to find out whether the purposes are being achieved.[12] Accountability is undeniably important; we need to make sure that things that need doing get done. But as the old adage has it, "too much of a good thing can hurt you." Bringing out divergent views can make the competition for scarce resources more intense and acrimonious. Needed work may go undone due to such conflicts. Thus clarifying goals may serve neither accountability nor effectiveness. Better than the injunction to "clarify your goals" would be the encouragement to consider the tradeoff between increased accountability and decreased effectiveness.[13]

What is an Activity? What is a Function?

Once objectives have been clarified, ZBB requires that managers divide up their activities into a series of decision packages which then become the building blocks of the organization's budget.

People who write about implementing zero-base budgeting, however, pay very little attention to the political and organizational implications of defining activities one way or another. Peter Pyhrr, for instance, while recognizing that decision packages can be built in a multiplicity of ways, nevertheless believes that "... the subject of the package is immaterial. Managers should be interested only in the benefits achieved for a given expenditure . . ."[14] But in single-mindedly focusing on the costs and benefits of any given *expenditure*, ZBB advocates blind themselves to the *political* costs and benefits of categorizing any given *activity* in different ways.

Because objectives are multiple, and at times conflicting, different people will view the same activity in different ways. One way of grouping activities will be useful in the pursuit of one objective but not useful at all for other objectives. Categorizing an agency's activities by geography, for example, will enable us to distribute funds in a geographically equitable manner. It won't allow us to easily control how the funds are being spent in terms of functions such as personnel, administration, maintenance, construction, and so forth. For this reason, the simple act of categorizing can be a political tool useful for promoting or defending political interests.[15]

Let us give an example of how the Georgia Highway Patrol constructed its decision packages in the Carter Administration.[16] Pyhrr says that three basic alternatives were considered:

1. A series of decision packages for the Highway Patrol as a whole.
2. A series of decision packages for each Patrol post [there were forty-five] with a combination of functions in each package.
3. A series of decision packages for each function performed at each patrol post.

The Highway Patrol decided on the first alternative, a not unreasonable choice, and one of the benefits of the resulting analysis, according to Pyhrr and Carter, was the hiring of full-time clerk dispatchers and radio operators to relieve the troopers of periodic station duty manning the radios and doing other such chores.

The consequence of preparing decision packages by "function" for the Highway Patrol as a whole was to make comparisons among the forty-five Patrol posts virtually impossible. One standard cost-cutting practice (of whatever merit) is to close down and consolidate district offices into regional offices. A person seeking to keep open a post comparing unfavorably with other posts in workload, costs, or whatever would find it politically useful to have a functional, system-wide decision package format adopted. In this way, the central cost-cutters cannot identify the relative inefficiency of this post but must rely only on system-wide information.

There may well have been no attempt whatsoever to *conceal* differences in workload, costs and so forth among the posts. Our point is that the decision packages, as drawn up, provide no information one way or another. But had there been such a motive, precisely the same procedures would have been used—as a deliberate tactic. It is for these reasons that some administrators recognize the importance of *who it is* that prepares the decision packages, or at least determines the ground rules for their preparation.

One of the reasons for former Defense Secretary Robert McNamara's strength as an administrator in the Pentagon may have been the fact that it was McNamara and his civilian aides, and not the military services, who drew up the budgets' program categories.[17] Previously, budgetary problems and conflicts *within* a service could be settled without the Secretary of Defense ever being involved or aware; *interservice* rivalries, however, would come to his attention. The categories created and imposed on the Department of Defense budget by McNamara cut across organizational boundaries in a number of ways. Parts of both the Navy (its Polaris submarines) and the Air Force (its ICBM's and B-52's) were in the "Strategic and Retaliatory" program category, for example. With the imposition of these program categories, some conflicts that were previously only *intra-service* now became *inter-program* in addition, and were thus somewhat more likely to come to the attention of McNamara and his aides.[18] Had the services been left to their own devices, the "program" categories may simply have followed organizational boundaries. As a consequence, the political utility of strategically-chosen categories would have been lost. This is what happened in the U.S. Department of Agriculture's ineffective implementation of PPBS in the late 1960s. The USDA's agencies were allowed a great degree of discretion in devising their own program categories. The resulting categories strictly followed organizational boundaries, and they produced information only about problems and conflicts that the organizational structure itself was producing anyway; in consequence, program decisions continued to be made much as before.[19]

Whether decision packages should cut across or follow organizational lines depends upon the purpose for which information is gathered. If in the case of the Georgia Highway Patrol comparison among district Patrol posts is important for accountability, then collecting information by function system-wide does not serve that purpose. If a goal of the McNamara team was to make inter-program comparisons, then the program elements being scattered throughout the military service-based budget hindered the purpose. Only the program budget could ease such comparisons.

An additional aspect of this political process of creating and imposing categories has to do with the overall inclusiveness of the categories created. Programs can be defined in a very small, tight, and discrete manner, or they can be defined very broadly and vaguely. The U.S. Department of Agriculture gradually discovered this in its use of PPBS in the 1960s, according to Nienaber and Wildavsky's account.[20] Write the authors:

> The Department of Agriculture soon learned some of the basic political lessons involving the choice of program categories. Because the categories involved policy preferences, they had to be negotiated with each and every bureau. Initially, it seemed that the larger the number of categories, the easier the task of negotiation because the extent of conflict was minimized. Only later did the department learn that it was possible to move in the opposite direction with even greater effect. For if the number of categories was reduced to a basic minimum—say, three or four—they would become so large, include so heterogeneous a collection of elements, that they would not commit anyone to anything. It was only possible to get agreement on a set of categories either so numerous that they precluded comparison or so few as to lack specificity. Once that lesson had been learned, once the political nature of the categories had become manifest through experience, the department set about using its program categories to build support for its policies.[21]

So not only does the nature of the categories—function versus area, for example—have political meaning, but so does the sheer inclusiveness of the categories.

Both Peter Pyhrr and the OMB, however, seem unaware of all this. The OMB ZBB guidelines, for example, simply state that "to the extent possible, [the decision units should] reflect existing program and organizational structures that have accounting support."[22] The Public Health Service in HEW, for example, hewed close to the line: "Decision units were either existing budget line items or in combination with other decision units totaled to budget line items."[23] The Department of Defense adopted a decision unit structure which was based on aggregations of existing investment line items and operating organizations from its ongoing PPB process.[24] That agencies and departments such as these followed OMB's requirement without apparent objection suggests that they found the resulting categorizations to be politically congenial. On top of this, most agencies and departments created very broad and inclusive categories right at the outset. While this was done, by most accounts, in order to avoid creating huge numbers of packages,[25] top management and the OMB were left in a position in which only highly aggregated information was available. Without greater specificity, informed choices were difficult to make.

Not all participants found the recommended categories useful, however. While the new, activist leaders of ACTION (which houses the Peace Corps and other volunteer programs) accepted their agency's existing organization structure and accounting and information systems as "the logical building blocks" to be used for budget presentation to the OMB, they found that their own management goals were not helped. The new director wanted to shift his agency's focus of attention from the volunteers to the work the volunteers did for the people they served. But since these organization and information systems "did not adequately represent the new administration's goals, it was decided to build an internal system based on a categorization of the ways in which volunteer services meet basic human needs."[26] In this case, agency leaders seemed aware of the political implications of how categories are drawn: OMB's preference for existing budgetary structures did not mesh with their own internal management strategies, so a second budgeting system had to be drawn up.

In a similar case, OMB staffers sought to play a role in developing standard decision units for all National Foreign Intelligence Program components. The rationale, in the words of the two staffers involved, was that "we could better insure that certain program areas were given appropriate visibility in the budget, and the potential for cross-program analyses was enhanced."[27] We couldn't have put it any better ourselves; if those who drafted the OMB's ZBB guidelines were not aware of the political implications of budget categories, at least some of their assistants were.

In sum, how we prepare decision packages—that is, how we create categories to structure information—is dependent on what our *purposes* are in so doing. Some categories conceal; others will reveal. Some categories foster certain kinds of comparisons; others foster other kinds of comparisons. The decision to conceal or reveal information, and to foster some kinds of comparisons rather than others, is dependent on our purposes. In one organization functional categories may expose politically important information, while in another organization the same categories may hide such information. There exists, in other words, no hard and fast rule as to what the "best" categories are. This may explain the remarkable fact that the OMB guidelines nowhere discuss whether (much less how) objectives are to influence the drawing up of the decision package categories, despite the guidelines' recommendation that clarification of objectives be one of ZBB's starting points.

Whatever the reason, there is simply no recognition that the twin injunctions—to clarify objectives and to use traditional budget ac-

counts—might work contrary to each other. Thus when managers in
the "gut level" of an organization are given the freedom to formulate
decision packages as they see fit, the OMB is unwittingly exposing
zero-base budgeting to the risk of political manipulation at the very
beginning of the process. When, on the other hand, categories are
imposed by the OMB, as in the example just cited, ZBB thereby loses
much of the "grass roots" character prized by some of its proponents.

Pointing out this dilemma is not particularly novel, for it is part and
parcel of the age-old problem of managing large organizations. The
noteworthy point is that zero-base budgeting, its pretensions to the
contrary, hasn't somehow cut this Gordian knot.

On the Use of "Performance Measures" in Governmental Organizations

For so it is, oh Lord my God, I can measure it,
but what it is that I measure I do not know.[28]
St. Augustine

One of the claims made for zero-base budgeting is that it enables
managers to measure the performance of their operations. Pyhrr, for
example, in referring to managers who "place high priority on sur-
vival," and who survive by "keeping low profiles or 'keeping their
noses clean,' " tells us that:

> Zero-base budgeting takes away the blanket of security from these man-
> agers, *identifies exactly what and how well each activity is doing*, and
> forces some very difficult decisions.[29]

The Office of Management and Budget's 1977 guidelines on zero-
base budgeting to the executive departments also state that, ". . .
managers should . . . determine the key indicators by which performance and results are to be measured."[30]

Even if there were no problems of evaluation and measurement,
there is a wide variety of different ways of evaluating activities. One
could build very *efficient* dams, for example, with high benefit/cost
ratios; but this does *not* necessarily mean that lots of water is stored.
The measure for that would be some sort of *extensiveness* measure,
numbers of acre-feet in storage, for example. Nor do either of these
measures necessarily tell us anything about their *effectiveness*, that is,
are the purposes for which the water was stored actually accom-

plished? Finally, we might wonder whether the dam produces an *equitable* distribution of benefits, that is, is it socially or politically valuable?[31]

In such a project, we might find that each of these measures has a champion. The Office of Management and Budget might value a high benefit/cost ratio. Irrigators and water recreation enthusiasts might value a very large reservoir. The congressional appropriations committees might be most concerned about the effectiveness of the project, while the authorizing committees and the President might focus on the distribution of project benefits. What is needed is mutual agreement among the efficiency advocates, the agriculturalists and the recreationists, the congressional committees and the President. Maximizing on any one dimension produces, in effect, a non-negotiable demand that others must adjust to this one interest. If evaluators only consider one dimension, they miss the inherently political and negotiable character of the adjustment process. Trading off the efficiency of one kind of dam versus the equitability of another structure is not something that can be decided by reference to an economic formula.[32]

In a sense, these detailed points on how to measure government benefits are beside the point. For of the numerous sample decision packages displayed by Pyhrr, Cheek, and the other ZBB commentators, seldom are *anything* more than "extensiveness" and "efficiency" measures used. Moreover, the efficiency measures are simply items such as cost per air pollution sample taken, derived merely by dividing the total cost of running the air pollution laboratory by the number of air samples taken.[33] In other words, what Schick described as characteristic of performance budgeting—the use of only extensiveness and efficiency measures—is also characteristic of ZBB.[34] Otherwise, why would Pyhrr use this example?[35]

What was descriptive of ZBB in Georgia is already apparently true of the federal government's effort. In the OMB Bulletin instructing the agencies how to implement ZBB, the example used is the dispensation by HEW of federal money to Community Mental Health Centers around the country. Although the OMB's sample decision packages tell us that these centers provide services such as inpatient hospitalization, outpatient counseling, and alcohol and drug abuse programs, the *only* quantitative measures employed are numbers of centers of various types, number of centers receiving federal grants, percent of "population covered," and percent of "probable patients covered."[36] These are *at best* extensiveness measures. There is not even a word about efficiency of any kind, much less measures of effectiveness or anything else. This example is, we note, a product of the agency which is overseeing the implementation of ZBB. It is not an auspicious beginning.

Even when quantitative measures are not available, agencies are exhorted by the OMB to try to create them anyway:

> If such [evaluation and workload measurement] systems do not exist, or if data are not readily available, desirable performance indicators should not be rejected because of apparent difficulties in measurement. Indirect or proxy indicators should be considered initially, while evaluation and workload systems are developed to provide the necessary data for subsequent budget cycles.[37]

Creating indirect or proxy indicators is not an uncommon or unwise thing to do.[38] But common usage does not necessarily indicate easy interpretation or accurate results. The more indirect the indicator, the greater the caution required in interpreting the results they give. Among the best such indicators are those which the "subject" does not know are being used. This is seldom if ever the case with their use in governmental organizations.

The "squishier" the field in which they are being used, the more likely it is that a whole family of indirect or proxy indicators will be required in order to compensate for the defects in any one of them.[39] But this also means a good probability of their indicating quite different things.[40] One can therefore expect a self-interested agency to use the most "favorable" indicators in its decision packages, and simply not report the others.[41] (These unfavorable indicators may continue to be used on an informal basis by the agency's managers for their own purposes, though the possibility of such information being leaked does remain. Agencies can be expected to do their best self-evaluations for themselves; self-evaluations for others is always problematical.)[42]

If indirect or proxy indicators are required of an agency, and higher-level decisions about the agency are actually premised on what the indicators "reveal," then we can expect "goal displacement" to occur. That is, the agency will orient its behavior toward looking good on the proxy indicators, rather than toward what it is that the indicator is supposed to be a measure of.[43] Numerous examples from the daily life of ordinary organizations can be cited.

Police departments may feel an incentive to issue numerous traffic tickets (one often hears allegations about "quotas" being required of patrolmen) rather than focusing energies on the prevention of serious crimes. Health Maintenance Organizations (HMOs) may find it to their advantage to "skim" the best, that is, healthiest, members of a community, who are usually the middle-aged, middle-class, leaving the neediest of the aged and the poor without their services. In the late 1960s the use of private firms to run schools was the rage, in part since the firms were willing to sign "performance contracts" guaranteeing that their students would pass certain standardized tests. Then it was discovered that some of them were having their students spend inordinate amounts of time practicing test-taking. Goal displacement was at work.

At a broader level Navasky suggests in his book on the Attorney Generalship of Robert Kennedy[44] that J. Edgar Hoover deliberately focused the FBI's activities on car thefts, bank robberies, and kidnappings, and avoided organized crime and southern civil rights violations because the FBI could look good on the former, relatively easy-to-solve crimes, with minimal risks of corruption or political backlash, but probably would not have looked as good on the latter. One can "skim" crime as well as healthy patients.

Jimmy Carter should be well aware of the misuse of performance measures by government agencies. In his autobiography *Why Not The Best?* he describes his experiences with the Army Corps of Engineers concerning a dam on the Flint River in Georgia. Although he initially supported the dam, public opposition manifested itself and he was prevailed upon to take a closer look at the Corps' justification for the project as contained in its benefit/cost calculations. As he puts his findings:

> Exaggerated claims for benefits were combined with shrunken costs estimated to justify the project. . . . Population figures for future years in the area in the Corps' report had been strangely doubled, electrical power generators would have to run at more than 125 percent capacity. . . . Flood control benefits had been increased by a factor of 287 percent since the initial estimates. . . . In just a few months the Corps more than quadrupled the economic benefits from recreation, and federal recreational advantages computed by the Corps were 1,650 percent more than those which had been originally computed by the National Park Service.[45]

Now in this case, it took a considerable amount of digging to uncover the phony statistics, and the General Accounting Office had to be called in to examine the Corps' figures. But there were 10,000 decision packages in Georgia under Carter's ZBB; the idea of investigating each decision package for numbers fraud, much less deciding what to do about it when discovered in the midst of budget preparation, boggles the mind.[46]

Allen Schick once commented that ". . . data are not neutral elements of budgetary mechanics but instruments of power in budgeting and appropriations."[47] This is true no matter what budgeting technique is employed. ZBB proponents neither discuss this issue nor provide examples showing a sensitivity to it. In fact, by requiring a *single* standardized measurement for the decision package—the examples given are almost always just extensiveness or efficiency measures, and not true effectiveness measures—they may have made political manipulation easier. This should be an unsettling thought for those who believe that ZBB reduces the influence of politics on budgetary decisions.

What Use are Most Performance Measures, or "Who the Hell Cares How Much a Pound of Laundry Costs?"[48]

Even if we believe performance measures to be valid and accurate, they still require considerable interpretation before we know what to do with them. Numbers have no intrinsic meaning. They have meaning only in some context. For budgeters, "context" implies either historical context or theoretical context. Theoretical context is lacking for a great many policy problems. That is why we invest time and money in policy research. Pending results from this research, we are left in most cases with historical context, and under reasonably stable conditions, there is no better measure of what $110 million will produce in a program than the knowledge of what $100 million produced last year. But this is exactly what traditional incremental budgeting is all about, and exactly what ZBB proponents denigrate.

So under most conditions, performance measures can only be used as part of a historical time-series of data. Even then, a historical trend in a body of data still requires considerable evaluation. How should the governor of Georgia react, for example, to the fact that the cost of an air pollution sample has gone from $4.07 to $3.75? It is not immediately obvious what this means, if anything. Does it mean that efficiency is increasing? Probably not, if the quality or reliability of testing has gone down; what if there is no indicator that will alert him to quality or reliability changes in the decision packages?

If, for some reason, a budget official perusing the indicators in a decision package comes to feel that the program is "inefficient" or whatever, there are still several possible (and conflicting) ways in which the indicators might be interpreted:

- It might be that the task is intrinsically difficult, and that it simply takes numerous inputs in order to get any output. But the task might still be worthwhile.

- It might be that the task is intrinsically difficult, and it is not worthwhile engaging in it because it can't be done, or it can't be done at "reasonable" cost.
- It might be that the task is difficult, and perhaps with increased research expenditures would be more easily accomplished.

Performance measures in and of themselves thus don't provide the clues as to how they should be interpreted.[49]

Even having some elements of a *theory* of how benefits are produced by expenditures doesn't necessarily tell us what to do. If we know, for example, that the production rate of benefits from a given program increases temporarily with more expenditures, then levels off at some plateau, and finally begins to decline, accurate measures of both benefits and expenditures might not tell us which way to move if we don't know where we are on the curve, and which curve we are on. Let's look at Figure 1 for an example. Not only do we have to know where we *are*, that is, how much we are spending and what we are getting for the expense (Point X in the Figure), but we also have to know which curve we are on—is it curve A, B, or C?

Figure 1

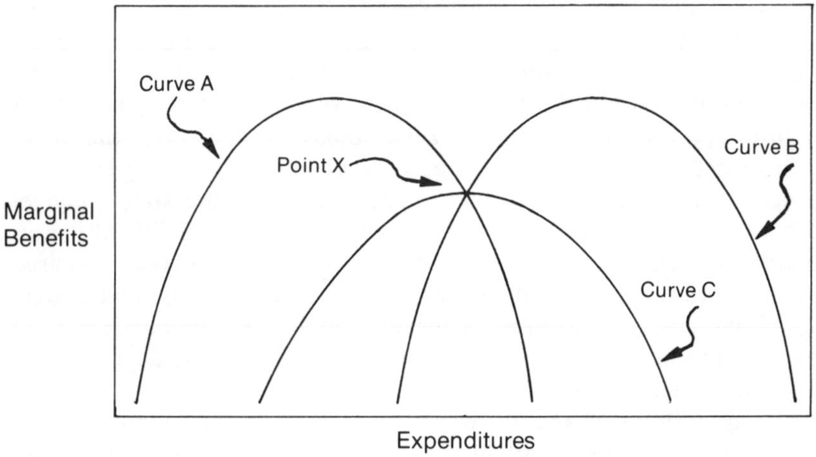

Point X is one's observed expenditures and benefits derived therefrom. Question: Are we on curve A (then decrease expenditures to become more efficient), or are we on curve B (then increase expenditures to become more efficient), or are we on curve C (then stay where we are)?

In the absence of such a verified theory—what are the shapes of the curves, what curve are we on, and where are we on the curve?—which we can use to guide our behavior, we will almost invariably end up using our "understanding" of the "context" of our problem, and of what the "historical trends" appear to be. This is why the decision packages almost always show these performance measures as part of a historical series of such numbers, and not just one year's worth. The kind of behavior which would appear to be "rational" under such circumstances is to take small, iterative steps one at a time in plausible directions and to check what the consequences are afterwards.

Amusingly, Pyhrr seems to sanction such incrementalism, despite his brave words about ZBB telling us "exactly what and how well each activity is doing." For in discussing how a firm's "profit plan" will be put together under zero-base budgeting, he states that it is an "iterative decision making process where management can be guided by models or historical trends in establishing profit levels for each organizational unit."[50] Iteration and the use of historical trends, both prime elements of incrementalism, appear to be integral to ZBB also.

What is the actual experience with attempting to gather such data? In many cases, the numbers are not available, and even when they are available, they are of questionable utility. The experiences of Georgia are instructive. The state has oscillated back and forth over the question of how much quantitative data should be gathered, and over the question of what to do with the numbers when they were generated.[51]

In the preparation of the first ZBB budget, for FY 1973, the quantitative data desired were lacking. This was understandable since the process was new. Without such data, analysts in the state's budget office (the Office of Planning and Budget, the OPB) had difficulty evaluating the packages. As a result, the 1974 budget instructions required much more quantitative data than the 1973 instructions, and budget forms were revised to provide the needed space. The changes were expected to increase both the amount and quality of the data, thereby allowing easier evaluation.

Things didn't work out this way. The changes, according to Minmier, "did not produce the desired result but rather created additional problems . . ."[52] One problem was the great amount of time required to collect detailed cost information for the decision packages. And in most cases, said Minmier, the cost data "simply was not available."[53] As a consequence, he continued, "most costs assigned to a decision package were a result of an arbitrary allocation of the activity's costs."[54]

Most departmental budget analysts and fiscal officers felt that the detailed cost data in their own decision packages were "virtually useless."[55] One analyst commented, for example, that ". . . the cost data we use on the packages are estimates and in some cases have very little meaning." A second even confessed that "[t]he amounts shown on decision packages are mathematical calculations to arrive at a predetermined figure for the activity."[56] The budget analysts in the Office of Planning and Budget agreed; one comment exemplified their views: "We realized that the cost data in the decision package was inaccurate. Therefore we just ignored it."[57]

Had such detailed cost information been worthwhile to collect, that is, had the data been expected to serve a useful purpose, we would have expected the OPB to persevere despite the collection difficulties. But in fact, the decision was made to *eliminate* the requirement for detailed cost measures at the decision package level for the FY 1975 budget. Henceforth, such costs were to be accumulated at the "activity" level, the next level of aggregation above the functional decision packages as they had been previously prepared. Three years later, however, the pendulum was apparently swinging back again, for Schick and Keith report that the latest budget instructions required Georgia's agencies to submit to the OPB a list of performance measures to be used for each function performed.[58]

How were these data actually used? Minmier did not pursue this question, but there are hints in his study that the data were not in fact used much. One departmental budget analyst, for example, commented that ". . . those making the final decision do not use the information." A second claimed that analysts in the OPB did not have the time to carefully examine decision packages "[b]ecause of all the detail required..."[59] Minmier himself observed that "it is also the conclusion based on this study that many of the department heads have not utilized this new management information."[60]

Although Minmier does not discuss the question, it seems probable that there was little agreement on—or even awareness of—the purposes of collecting these performance measures. With better awareness of purpose, we might have seen a more sustained effort to solve the problems of gathering the data. Even Peter Pyhrr warns that it may take several years to develop adequate information gathering systems.[61] Without some reasonably well-understood purpose, however, ever more detailed data collection can become a mindless exercise. In Hogan's study of zero-base budgeting in Texas, this issue is confronted directly.[62]

Hogan notes that while the Governor and Lieutenant Governor knew they wanted ZBB implemented, what they wanted it implemented *for*

remained unclear. The type of information desired by these two officials, said Hogan, "was never fully communicated to the staff beyond
the point that 'all governmental services should be justified . . .' "
Performance measures and so forth were adopted, but what was not
evident "was how decision-makers wished to see such information
displayed. For some reason, this never became clear during the entire
process."[63]

Without guidance as to what to look for, the Texas budget examiners,
who were "struggling to filter through the substantial amount of additional information," soon found that their problems "were compounded when they were confronted with the responsibility of
structuring the information in such a manner so that it would be relevant to decision-makers." But without

> . . . any definite indication of the desires of the Governor or members of
> the Legislature, they were left with the most difficult task of either an-
> ticipating informational needs and proceeding accordingly or presenting
> information in the same manner that was most meaningful to them
> (examiners).

As a result, concluded Hogan, "examiners felt a real sense of frustration . . ."[64]

Little evidence is yet available on ZBB's use of performance measures in the federal government. In the largest compilation of reports
on ZBB's use there, scarcely any mention was made of this aspect of
ZBB.[65] When mention was made, as in the case of the Small Business
Administration, it was found that "In most instances, program managers did not have the benefit of effectiveness evaluations relating to
the decision units. . . . [D]ata necessary for that purpose just were not
available to the program managers."[66] Whether the needed measures
could and would be forthcoming is difficult to predict.

Do these performance measures in zero-base budgeting, then, tell us
"exactly what and how well each activity is doing"? Not by a long
shot. If carefully interpreted, quantified performance measures can
serve useful purposes; if they can be useful, there is no reason not to
collect them. But there are strong arguments against their uniform
requirement from all expenditure programs. No matter what the budgetary technique, it is difficult to gather such numbers; when they are
gathered, they become susceptible to political manipulation; if the measures are indirect of proxy measures, goal displacement may result;
and even when the numbers are trustworthy, few people may know
what to do with them. The federal ZBB instructions, moreover, give
no guidance on how to overcome these problems.

Notes

1. Defining rationality in this way may cause some discomfort. As Nagle commented in his review of Pyhrr's 1973 book: "The model that Pyhrr presents seems too rational to challenge. How can you argue with it? Indeed, the key to challenging the model can be found by examining the real world application of ZBB." Jim Nagle, "Zero Base Budgeting," *The Bureaucrat* 6 (Spring 1977), p. 154. We do just this in Chapters 2, 3, and 4. In Chapter 5, however, we do challenge the model on theoretical grounds.

2. On performance budgeting and program budgeting in state governments, see Allen Schick, *Budget Innovation in the States* (Washington D.C.: The Brookings Institution, 1971). On program budgeting in the federal government, see Aaron Wildavsky, *Budgeting* (Boston: Little, Brown, 1975), chapters 13-18, and Jeanne Nienaber and Aaron Wildavsky's detailed case study of program budgeting in the Forest Service and National Park Service, *The Budgeting and Evaluation of Federal Recreation Programs, or Money Doesn't Grow On Trees* (New York: Basic Books, 1973). For Management-by-Objectives see Joel Havemann, "OMB Begins Major Program to Identify and Attain Presidential Goals," *National Journal* 9 (2 April 1977): 514-517; and Richard Rose, *Managing Presidential Objectives* (New York: The Free Press, 1976).

3. Bulletin No. 77-9, Office of Management and Budget, in *The Federal Register*, April 19, 1977, p. 22342.

4. In a recent article on Management-by-Objectives (MBO), Peter Drucker, management theorist and consultant, pointed out that objectives in public service agencies are "ambiguous, ambivalent, and multiple. This holds true in private business as well." See his "What Results Should You Expect? A User's Guide to MBO," *Public Administration Review* 36 (January/February 1976), p. 13.

5. See, for example, Jules Witcover, *Marathon* (New York: The Viking Press, 1977), pp. 515-516, 579-583. See also James T. Wooten, "Carter's Campaign Is Producing A Broad Range of Impressions," *The New York Times*, February 11, 1976 and "Carter's Way With Issues Bothers Voters," *The New York Times*, March 15, 1976.

6. Charles Lindblom was perhaps the first person to argue for leaving goals ambiguous as long as participants could agree on policies. He advises that "In collective decision-making, do not try to clarify values if the parties concerned can agree on policies, as they often can, despite their disagreement on values." See his "Limitations on Rationality" in Carl J. Friedrich, ed., *Rational Decisions, Nomos*, Vol. VII (New York: Atherton Press, 1964), p. 227.

7. See Joel Havemann, "Administration Report/OMB Begins Major Program To Identify And Attain Presidential Goals," *National Journal* 5 (2 June 1973), p. 787.

8. See Richard M. Cyert and James G. March, *A Behavioral Theory of the Firm* (Englewood Cliffs, N.J.: Prentice-Hall, 1963), see pp. 36-38 for example.

9. This is admittedly not very heroic sounding. Jimmy Carter would not have sold many copies of his autobiography had it been titled *Why Not The Satisfactory?*

10. See Peter Drucker, "MBO—Tool or Master," *The Federal Accountant* 24 (September 1975), p. 24. Drucker later actually went so far as to say that what is required to understand complex issues is "informed dissent." See "What Results Should You Expect?" p. 17.

11. It is often said that the profit motive instills one singular goal in business-men. A corollary is that businesses don't have multiple or conflicting goals. If this were descriptively accurate, then MBO need not have been invented for businessmen. But it was invented. Joseph Bower tells us in his study of corporate resource allocation decisions that ". . . the objectives of man-agement of a large organization . . . are not in any way a sufficient de-scription of the objectives which direct and motivate action at the critical, resource allocating levels of the organization." Instead, matters are much more complex, for Bower commented that, "Perhaps the most striking aspect of the process of resource allocation . . . is the extent to which it is more complex than most managers seem to believe. . . . [W]e have found capital investment to be a process of study, bargaining, persuasion and choice spread over many levels of the organization and over long periods of time." See Joseph L. Bower, *Managing the Resource Allocation Process* (Boston: Harvard Business School, 1970), pp. 17, 320-321.

12. Thirty years ago, in his *An Introduction to Legal Reasoning* (Chicago: University of Chicago Press, 1949), Edward H. Levi described the prob-lems such ambiguity posed for judicial interpretation of statutes. (See pp. 21-22). Courts—as evaluators—have long faced the same problems that contemporary reformers newly decry.

13. Again, Peter Drucker has ultimately come to the same kind of conclusion: ". . . the most important result of management by *objectives* is that it forces the administrator into the realization that there cannot be one single objective . . . [R]ealization of this fundamental problem . . . forces the administrator and his agency to a realization of the need to think and of the need to make highly risky balancing and tradeoff decisions." See "What Results Should You Expect?" p. 14, emphasis in original. Unfor-tunately, ZBB (and MBO) tell us nothing about *how* to make these tradeoffs better.

14. Pyhrr, *Zero-Base Budgeting*, p. 51.

15. Wildavsky flatly states that "[c]ategories are strategies . . ." in his discus-sion of PPBS in the Forest Service in the 1960s, in *Budgeting*, p. 276.

16. See Pyhrr, 1973, pp. 39-45.

17. Program categories in PPBS are in general broader than decision packages. But the "categories as strategies" ideas apply to both programs and de-cision packages.

18. Such redundant and overlapping budget and organizational categories ap-pear to be of considerable political utility. Unfortunately, Pyhrr and Carter stress the need for eliminating redundancy and overlap from government.

19. For an account of PPBS in the USDA, see Nienaber and Wildavsky, *The Budgeting and Evaluation of Federal Recreation Programs*, chapters 4 and 5.

20. Ibid, ch. 5.

21. Ibid, pp. 129-130.

22. OMB Bulletin, 77-9, p. 22343.
23. Tony Itteilag, "FY 1979 ZBB Formulation in the Public Health Service," *The Bureaucrat* 7 (Spring 1978), p. 16.
24. See John R. Quetsch, "ZBB and DoD," *The Bureaucrat* 7 (Spring 1978), p. 32.
25. See the comments by F. Dale Draper and Bernard T. Pitsvada, "Zero-Base Budgeting in the Federal Government; Some Preliminary Observations On The First Year's Effort," *The Government Accountants Journal* 27 (Spring 1978), p. 23.
26. Emerson Markham, "Zero-base Budgeting in ACTION," *The Bureaucrat* 7 (Spring 1978), p. 48.
27. Nanette M. Blandin and Arnold E. Donahue, "ZBB: Not A Panacea, But A Definite Plus," *The Bureaucrat* 7 (Spring 1978), p. 53.
28. Cited by Edward R. Tufte, "Political Statistics for the United States," *American Political Science Review* 71 (March 1977), p. 305.
29. Pyhrr, *Zero-Base Budgeting*, p. 27, emphasis added.
30. P. 22342.
31. Allen Schick uses this terminology in *Budget Innovation in the States*, p. 137.
32. It is possible that the *most efficient* dam will be one a hundred times as big as planned, because of economies of scale, for example. We may not, however, have enough money to build one so big. Can efficiency no longer be a goal in this case? Perhaps we should seek to build the biggest dam for a given amount of money? But how will the central budget office know how much money to give us if we can't tell them what benefits to expect, because we don't know how big a dam we will be allowed to build?
33. This particular air pollution laboratory example crops up in the ZBB literature frequently. (See references below). Pyhrr shows it in his book (pp. 38-39), Granof and Kinzel use it as an example of a decision package (pp. 51-52), and Minmier uses it twice (p. 8 of *The Government Accountants Journal* article and pp. 52-53 of his longer study of ZBB in Georgia). Why such a poor example of benefit/cost analysis should be so proudly displayed is a mystery. The example gives us no idea whatsoever of the actual benefits of taking various numbers of air pollution samples. All we are told, as an example of "benefit/cost" analysis, is the cost per sample and the percentage of Georgia's population included in sampling areas.
   See Peter Pyhrr, "The Zero-Base Approach to Government Budgeting"; Michael H. Granof and Dale A. Kinzel, "Zero-Based Budgeting: Modest Proposal For Reform," *The Federal Accountant* 23 (December 1974); George S. Minmier and Roger Hermanson, "A Look At Zero-Based Budgeting: The Georgia Experience," *The Government Accountants Journal* 25 (Winter 1976-77); George S. Minmier, *An Evaluation of the Zero-Base Budgeting System in Governmental Institutions* (Atlanta, Georgia: School of Business Administration, Georgia State University, 1975), reprinted in U.S. Senate Subcommittee on Intergovernmental Relations of the Committee on Governmental Operations, *Compendium of Materials on Zero-Base Budgeting in the States* (Washington D.C.: U.S. Government Printing Office, 1977). This collection is hereafter referred to as "Compendium."
34. See *Budget Innovation in the States*, p. 59.

35. After three years of experience with ZBB in New Mexico, LaFaver wrote in 1974: "Without a great deal of care, performance measures often show how busy people are rather than the cost-benefit of their activity." John LaFaver, "Zero-Base Budgeting in New Mexico," *State Government* 47 (Spring 1974), p. 112. Georgia is evidently not unique.
36. See OMB Bulletin 77-9, p. 22348.
37. P. 22342 of the OMB Bulletin.
38. We might note that these proxy indicators may be as necessary in the private sector as in the public sector. As Verne Lewis pointed out in his well-known 1952 article on alternative budgeting schemes: "In attempting to calculate whether a given activity will yield a profit, a businessman, however, faces some of the problems faced by government. He has to forecast market conditions. The numbers he forecasts may or may not be right. Likewise, a businessman cannot always determine even after the fact whether an individual activity has been profitable or not. No method has yet been found, for example, of measuring precisely how much of a company's profit or loss results from such activities as advertising, research, and employee welfare programs. Moreover, a businessman, if he wants to maximize profits, cannot engage in an activity just because it is profitable. It must be more profitable than alternative activities open to him. Thus, he is faced with the same problem of relative value as is the government official." See "Toward A Theory Of Budgeting," *Public Administration Review* 12 (Winter 1952), p. 47.
39. There's that nasty redundancy again, though.
40. There are some limits to the utility of proxy indicators. Congressman Max Baucus (D-Montana) asked the head of the Consumer Product Safety Commission, with some exasperation, about the quality of the CPSC evaluation measures. After one of their responses, he retorted, "Have you tried any other evaluation measures besides whether everybody is happy?" U.S. House of Representatives, Hearings Before the Subcommittee on Appropriations, "Part 4: Consumer Product Safety Commission," 95th Congress, First Session, March 16-17, 1977 (Washington D.C.: U.S. Government Printing Office, 1977), p. 109.
41. Harold Wilensky's *Organizational Intelligence* (New York: Basic Books, 1967) is devoted to the study of how organizations can distort information for their various and sundry purposes.
42. On this point see Wildavsky, "The Self-Evaluating Organization," *Public Administration Review* 32 (September/October 1972): 509-520.
43. Harold Lasswell once remarked that "the human animal distinguishes himself by his infinite capacity for making ends of his means." Cited by Robert K. Merton in "Bureaucratic Structure and Personality," in Robert K. Merton, Ailsa P. Gray, Barbara Hockey, and Hanan C. Selvin, editors, *Reader in Bureaucracy* (Glencoe, Ill.: The Free Press of Glencoe, 1952), p. 365.
44. *Kennedy Justice* (New York: Atheneum, 1971), chapters 1-3.
45. (Nashville, Tenn.: Broadman Press, 1975), pp. 136-137.
46. Regarding the data from the popular Georgia air pollution example, it might be quite easy to produce an "increased" efficiency—i.e., the cost per sample taken—of almost any desired magnitude, as long as samples are reasonably quick and easy to take. All that would need to be done at each

sampling station is to take a few "extra" samples each day. "Efficiency" would appear to increase, though of course these extra samples might be doing no one any good.

47. *Budget Innovation in the States*, p. 189.
48. A comment made by a New York State legislator about the mass of un-informative data contained in a performance budget submitted to the leg-islature. Quoted by Schick, *Budget Innovation in the States*, p. 65.
49. Scheiring's comments about New Jersey's experiences with ZBB may be relevant here: "An additional problem was the lack of staff time and qual-ified staff to do proper program analysis of the decision packages. In many cases, zero-base [budgeting] served to highlight the program problems, issues, and alternatives which only accented management's perplexities in trying to find needed solutions." See Michael J. Scheiring, "Zero-Based Budgeting in New Jersey," in *Compendium*, p. 378.
50. Pyhrr, *Zero-Base Budgeting*, pp. 98-99. It is interesting to remind ourselves that these theories of limited rationality and sequential, incremental de-cision-making were developed in part by social scientists (such as Cyert and March) who were working at understanding the behavior of *business* organizations.
51. See George Minmier, *An Evaluation of the Zero-Base Budgeting System in Governmental Institutions*. This is by far the best study of ZBB in action, and we rely on it heavily in the pages to come. It is particularly useful since it covers the adoption and use of ZBB by Governor Jimmy Carter in Georgia from 1971 to 1975. At some points our interpretations of Minmier's data diverge from his own; we try to indicate where this is the case. Overall, we should note, Professor Minmier remains an advocate of a simplified and modified version of ZBB.
52. Minmier, p. 99.
53. Ibid, p. 101.
54. Ibid, p. 101.
55. Ibid, p. 102.
56. Ibid, p. 260, 259.
57. Ibid, p. 102.
58. Allen Schick and Robert Keith, "Zero Base Budgeting In The States," (1976), in *Compendium*, p. 35.
59. Minmier, pp. 261, 264.
60. Ibid, p. 167.
61. See Pyhrr, 1973, ch. 2, for example.
62. See Roy Lee Hogan, "Zero-Base Budgeting: A Rationalistic Attempt to Improve the Texas Budget System," (University of Texas, Austin: unpub-lished Master's Thesis in Public Administration, December 1975). Chap-ters 5, 6 and 7 are reprinted in *Compendium*, pp. 224-317. All page references to Hogan refer to this latter source.
63. Hogan, pp. 270-271 in *Compendium*.
64. Hogan, pp. 270-271 in *Compendium*.
65. See *The Bureaucrat* 7 (Spring 1978) "Forum" on ZBB.
66. Herbert T. Mills, "Zero-base Budgeting: The Initial Experience in SBA," *The Bureaucrat* 7 (Spring 1978), p. 29.

Chapter 3

Planning Plus Scarce Resources Equals Budgeting

We have not yet said much about budgeting. We have only discussed activities and decision packages, performance measures, and objective setting. By themselves, these are all just exercises in planning. Not until money and other scarce resources enter the scene can we call the process *budgeting*.

Does ZBB Separate Planning from Budgeting?

One of the supposed merits of ZBB is that it *integrates* planning and budgeting. Both Peter Pyhrr and another ZBB proponent, Logan Cheek,[1] accuse incremental budgeting of separating planning and budgeting. But a careful analysis of ZBB's procedures reveals that it is ZBB—not incremental budgeting—that divorces planning from budgeting. Two related issues are involved. The first is the question of just how decision packages are formulated, and the second is the question of whether or not the agency is provided with expenditure guidelines.

Two kinds of alternatives are to be considered when decision packages are formulated. On the one hand, we must note several different ways (methods, approaches) of accomplishing a given task. On the other hand, we must envision different amounts of money being spent on each way of accomplishing the task. Pyhrr and Cheek and other ZBB commentators suggest that we should *first* choose our preferred way of accomplishing a task, and *only then* should we concern ourselves with how much money to spend carrying out the task in this preferred way. If one were to design a way to *separate* planning from budgeting, this would be it. Suppose a person plans a data processing center, for example, without knowing how much money is either available or likely to be. If he lays plans for an IBM 370, and then receives

33

a budget sufficient to purchase an abacus, three slide rules and a pocket calculator, he will have wasted his time. The way people normally budget is somewhat different. They either choose a way of accomplishing a task while *simultaneously* (or iteratively) considering money available, or else they first tentatively budget a certain amount of money, and then examine and choose among the alternatives that are feasible within the constraint. This latter is, of course, the *reverse* of the recommended ZBB sequence.

Yet as far as we can tell, *first* choosing a method *and then* determining the money available is exactly what proponents of ZBB would have us do. Logan Cheek is the most forthright on the issue:

> Logic dictates that alternative *ways* be looked at first, choosing the best one of them. Then alternative *levels* are selected within the chosen way.[2]

Pyhrr comments in a 1977 article:

> *Once* the best method of accomplishing the operation has been chosen from among the various alternative methods evaluated, a manager must identify alternative levels of effort and funding to perform that operation.[3]

Only the OMB, in its "Zero-Base Budgeting" bulletin, appears to recognize that selecting an alternative has implications for the level of funding. It too cites this sequential process at first:

> Normally, the best alternative is then selected and used as the basis for the second type of analysis—the identification of different levels of funding, activity, or performance.[4]

But in the next paragraph the OMB appears to recognize that errors may be introduced:

> [P]ackages reflecting increased performance or funding levels may introduce alternative methods of accomplishment that were not feasible at a lower level.

This is the sole hint of recognition in the entire body of ZBB literature that there is a fallacy in the way decision packages are to be formulated.[5]

While not realizing they have created a problem, ZBB proponents nonetheless manage to propose a solution in the form of "expenditure guidelines." These guidelines, issued by the central budget office, tell the agency how much money it can expect to spend. Agency budgetary decisions are normally premised on such expectations. To zero-base

a budget, such expectations must be challenged. Examination and justification must take their place. But if agencies don't know how much
they are going to be allowed to spend, their planning takes place in a
vacuum, as we have just discussed. Peter Pyhrr strongly advises the
use of expenditure guidelines,[6] but their availability, however, invariably saps the strength of the "justify everything" injunction. A budget
put together using expenditure guidelines cannot be said to be a "zero-
base" budget. If headquarters has sent out a notice telling the agencies
what expenditure level to expect, a "justify everything anyway" request is little different from the standard "we remind you to be frugal"
homilies that central budget offices generally include in their
instructions.

Without expenditure guidelines, planning is divorced from budgeting. With the guidelines, planning and budgeting are reunited, but we
are left with traditional incremental budgeting. Since the guidelines *are*
normally used, as Peter Pyhrr advises,[7] preparation of ZBB's minimum-level-of-effort decision packages makes little sense. This suggests
that they deserve a closer look.

The Use—and Non-Use—of Minimum Level of Effort Decision Packages

The OMB bulletin on ZBB states that a "minimum" is:

> The program, activity, or funding level below which it is not feasible to
> continue the program, activity, or entity because no constructive con-
> tribution can be made toward fulfilling its objective.[8]

Left conveniently undefined are "feasible," "constructive," "contribution," "fulfilling," and "objective."

If the concept of a "minimum" is to have any meaning at all, budgeters must know the "production function" for an activity: that is, how
much output do we get for a given input?[9] But we can easily demon-
strate production functions where it is not all that clear what the "minimum" is. If, as we suspect, most government programs are
characterized by production functions as in Figure 1, then the conclusion must be that defining a "minimum" is essentially an arbitrary
process.[10]

Let's look at an example. Pick a civilian activity, *any* civilian activity
of the federal government. The odds are quite high that there is some
state, county, or city also engaging in this very same activity, but on
a vastly smaller scale. If some city is engaging in the activity, it is not

Figure 1

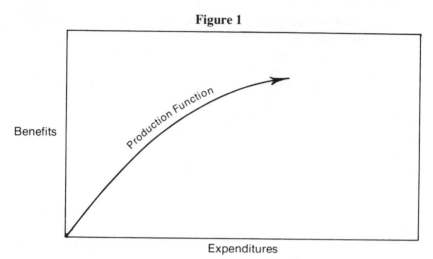

Benefits

Production Function

Expenditures

unreasonable to assume that the city is doing so for some rational reason. If a city finds it rational to engage in some activity, it is probable that the federal government will find it rational, too. Since the "minimum" of this city's activity is some fraction of current effort, we would therefore have to conclude that the "minimum" for the federal activity is the same size as the city's minimum for that activity. But this reduces federal "minimums" to an exceedingly small size, perhaps fractions of one percent of current activities; the utility of the concept diminishes accordingly.

What is the experience of states with the concept of the "minimum" package? Hogan's evidence from Texas shows that the role of the minimum package was different from that envisioned by the ZBB literature.[11] Although there were some differences in the views of agency personnel and central budget examiners, the "general consensus was that the minimum level was generally stated in a manner that tended to justify at least the current level of funding."[12] One agency official summarized such views by noting that the minimum level "appears to be an exercise of futility, costing the State much time and expense that could be utilized to *increase* the *current* performance level."[13]

Although in Texas a minimum level package had to be created at less than ninety percent of current funding, no instructions were offered to the agencies as to the number, size, or composition of their next increments. With no standard approach by the agencies, they did many different things. The examiners found it difficult to compare such incremental packages from different programs, and as a result, they "felt compelled to alter in some way the levels requested in formulating their recommendations," except when those levels represented "precisely the current level of funding."[14] As a consequence, Hogan noted, both agency personnel and budget office examiners were "almost unanimous" in desiring to see current-level-of-funding decision packages formulated by the agencies.[15] In light of his observations, Hogan concludes:

> Whatever can be said with regard to the identification of a current funding level being in conflict with the principles of zero-base budgeting, the simple fact remains that the current level of funding is important.[16]

The state of New Mexico had other difficulties with the concept.[17] In 1974 the state modified the zero-base procedures and no longer required the submission by the agencies of funding levels below last year's level. The main reason for the change was the extremely favorable economic forecasts for the coming years; some analysts predicted a surplus for the state of $100 million, nearly thirty percent of the current general fund budget. Under such generally favorable circumstances, LaFaver observes, ". . . it was obvious that the decision range for most budgets would be between 110 and 120 percent of present appropriations. Thus, there seemed to be little point in developing a 70 percent budget."[18]

In his study of Georgia, Minmier found the use of "minimums" to be little more useful than in Texas and New Mexico. Most decision packages did not vary much from one year to the next, and in particular, he found that the minimum level-of-effort decision packages "are merely duplicated each year after allowing for inflationary increases and increased workload."[19] Minmier also examined the FY 1973, 1974, and 1975 executive budgets to see what effect the minimum level packages had on these budgets, but discovered "[n]ot a single instance . . . where a function received less funds than it had in the previous fiscal year budget."[20] Nor did he find any functions that had received *only* those funds requested in the minimum level package. He learned instead that "all functions received the funds requested in the first incremental decision package to bring them to their current level of operations."[21] In the absence of a good theory describing what a "minimum" was and lacking guidelines as to how big minimums and increments should be, the bureaucrats in Georgia apparently behaved much as before.[22]

Further commentary on the difficulty of defining a minimum level of effort capability is provided by the congressional appropriations hearings on the National Aeronautics and Space Administration (NASA) budget requests in early 1977.[23] Congressman Max Baucus, a member of the House Appropriations subcommittee overseeing NASA's budget and its ZBB experiment, attempted to get the NASA comptroller, Mr. Elmer Groo, to state precisely what a "core capability"—essentially a minimum—for NASA would be. Groo had great difficulty. At one point he simply said, "I think you could get a different definition of what that would be from every individual who would respond to the question." Baucus pressed him again on the issue at a later point and Groo again expressed his discomfort with the concept: "I really do believe it is a matter of judgment. I don't think there's any final definition of a core capability at any given [space] center."[24]

What a "minimum" was troubled other departments and agencies during the drawing up of the FY 1979 federal budget. Two OMB budgeters summarized widespread sentiments when they noted that "the identification of a minimum decision package . . . is difficult both to conceptualize and implement." They also imply that some agencies tried to protect current resources in the minimum level packages, which, they suggest, brings us "right back to incremental budgeting."[25]

If few "natural" minimums can be found,[26] and if we still wish to create decision packages with less than current effort, it appears that we might have to impose some sort of *arbitrary* figure.[27] Peter Pyhrr, however, strongly advises against their use and recommends that "top management should take some other actions before falling back on such a poor solution."[28]

But "falling back" on arbitrary percentages appears to happen quite frequently in practice. Schick and Keith present data on the calculation of minimums in eleven states which are implementing ZBB in one form or another.[29] Of these eleven states, nine use either a fixed percentage of current expenditures as the "minimum," or else they use current expenditures themselves as the minimum. Of the two remaining states, Georgia instructed that a "minimum" shall merely be "below" the current funding level. Only Rhode Island of the eleven appeared to offer no guidance whatsoever. The OMB bulletin on ZBB specifies the same kind of minimum as Georgia's (as we might have expected). And in only two or three of these cases did instructions *not* suggest that the next incremental decision package bring the budget requests up to the current level.

The OMB bulletin on ZBB leaves specification of minimums as vague as they are in Georgia. In preparation of the FY 1979 budget, some forty percent of federal agencies apparently made good faith efforts at defining true minimums. The questionable character of these estimates, however, is suggested by the response by the Department of Housing and Urban Development to an OMB questionnaire on ZBB; setting minimum levels, said HUD, are "essentially, subjective judgments."[30] The remaining sixty percent of the federal agencies used an arbitrary percentage figure to establish the minimum, though the percentage of current budget varied from fifty to seventy-five percent as in the Environmental Protection Agency to ninety-five percent as in the Federal Maritime Commission; eighty-five percent and ninety-one percent were the most often used figures.[31]

Comments by the agencies showed the frustrations the concept posed. The budget director of the Small Business Administration, for example, noted that "It was difficult if not impossible for [program managers] to really develop a minimum level below which it would not be feasible to continue the program. Therefore, most minimum levels represented a predetermined percentage reduction and not a real analysis of the minimum level of the program."[32] The Environmental Protection Agency likewise found the formal definition of a minimum unworkable. One EPA official said that for many of its programs, "there is no clear level below which the programs would be useless." Arbitrarily defined minimums were used instead.[33] The Public Health Service made the same choice. Its budget director explained that the PHS "kept on falling into the trap of using an arbitrary percentage reduction below the current level when it couldn't otherwise establish the lowest feasible level to continue operations. In most programs, it is not known what the lowest feasible level is, and even if it were, no one, either in the executive branch or Congress, would want to implement it."[34]

Given the subjectivity involved in defining "minimums," agencies which in good faith do set relatively small minimums may be placing themselves at a disadvantage compared to those agencies establishing bigger minimums. If these two different sets of minimums are taken at face value by budget review personnel higher up, the first agency's requests may be placed in jeopardy: they simply will not look as important as those of the second agency.[35] As a result, we should expect to see an upward creep in the size of minimums over time, if they are treated seriously by top decision makers. The only way to avoid this would be for the OMB to explicitly set arbitrary percentages.

What do we make of the evidence on minimum level-of-effort decision packages? The use of arbitrary minimums—what Peter Pyhrr calls "such a poor solution"—appears to be remarkably prevalent in practice. It seems that the theoretical difficulties of defining a "minimum" are matched by the practical difficulties of actually defining them in the real world. Georgia has the longest experience with them, and the experience was poor enough to lead Minmier to recommend that they be prepared only once every four years, at the beginning of each new governor's term.[36] But Schick takes Minmier to task for this suggestion:

> Of course, the minimum-level packages are the distinctive "zero base" component of the system, and their elimination would convert the Georgia system into incremental budgeting.[37]

We agree.

If the "Minimums" Aren't Minimal, Are the "Alternatives" Alternative?

If governments cannot retrench to some elusive minimum, perhaps they can consider alternative methods for providing services, and thereby discover ways of doing things more efficiently and effectively. Zero-base instructions require, after all, that decision-makers develop and consider alternatives to the current way of doing things.

Hogan presents evidence on Texas that these alternatives did not play the role intended. The nine central budget office examiners he interviewed "expressed the general opinion" that the presentation of alternatives "did not prove useful to them in determining funding recommendations."[38] In fact, the examiners were also of the "nearly unanimous opinion" that the presentation of alternatives "was usually construed in such a manner so as to justify the present method of operation."[39] After examining a considerable number of decision packages, Hogan himself found that the number of times an alternative was used as the basis for a decision package was "zero."[40]

Several examples of cost-cutting in Georgia are often ascribed to the formal consideration of alternatives in ZBB: the use of fulltime clerk dispatchers/radio operators instead of Highway Patrolmen for H.P. administrative duties, the mowing of less grass along highways, the contracting out of fire fighting activities at state mental hospitals instead of maintaining the hospitals' own fire departments, and the firing of the state's six beekeepers.[41] Unfortunately, we have found no independent verification of how these changes came about and what the zero-base budgeting process had to do with their adoption.[42] Minmier does illustrate his report with several sample decision packages from Georgia and all, without exception, settle on the current way of doing things because the alternatives presented are either far too expensive, completely unrealistic, or both.[43]

Further indication that the alternatives generated in Georgia were little more realistic than those produced in Texas is given in the survey reported by Schick and Keith, who reveal that Georgia no longer requires the reporting of alternatives in the decision packages.[44]

Although there is not much evidence available, evaluations of the use of alternatives in the federal government suggest a similarly unencouraging picture. OMB staffers Blandin and Donahue describe the use of alternatives as an area of "relative weakness" in the ZBB effort.[45] One of the problems, as pointed out by the Public Health Service's budget director, was that "most real alternatives to current programs require major program changes and/or changes in legislation that cannot be accomplished within the budget year." He also commented that "there is not a realistic alternative for every ZBB decision unit."[46]

OMB's survey of the utility of formal consideration of alternatives produced statements from seventeen of seventy-three agencies that the process was helpful; some agencies even said that the alternatives were formally adopted. But as before, it is difficult to know whether these changes would have been made anyway, without the benefit of ZBB. This question the OMB did not ask. Some agencies which felt consideration of the alternatives was not useful commented that existing procedures already accomplished this same purpose.[47] Several agencies also argued that due to the time constraints of the budgetary process, there was not enough time to rethink ways of doing things. They noted in addition that objectives and alternatives tend to be related, and Draper and Pitsvada agreed, concluding that the consideration of alternatives "should precede budget preparation."[48]

The Difficulties of Ranking Decision Packages:
Volume, Incommensurability, and Politics

A central element of ZBB is the ranking of decision packages in order of priority. In the jargon of the trade, budgeters are to "prioritize" what they are doing and only provide money for those activities which are most important. Since resources are limited, budgeters must draw a cutoff line somewhere in the priority listing to separate those items getting funds from those which do not. It is at this point in the zero-base budgeting process that plans finally meet scarce resources.

What could be more sensible than deciding an agency's most important activities and then funding them? But deciding what is important is at the heart of budgeting; it cannot be relegated to a process in which budget items are simply listed in ordinal fashion. Showing us what is important is the task of the performance measures, and as we observed in our previous discussion, such measures are difficult to use, prone to political manipulation, difficult to interpret and likely to result in goal displacement. Moreover, programs often have multiple goals, which means measurement on multiple criteria if we are to rank packages. So before packages can be ranked, the criteria themselves must be ranked or assigned particular weights. But ranking criteria in order of priority may be even more difficult than ranking programs. How could someone decide whether *efficiency* should rank higher than *equity*, or *political popularity* lower than *economic merit?*

With such problems, how do budgeters actually manage to rank the numerous decision packages that are generated? The answer is, "only with great difficulty." In Georgia, for example, the ranking procedures were modified several times, and ultimately, the ranking requirement was more or less abandoned in favor of more traditional ways of doing things. Minmier describes what happened.

A "tremendous" but "unknown" number of decision packages was generated for the 1973 budget. Agency directors "constantly complained" of the large number of decision packages they were required to evaluate and rank.[49] To ease the problem for the 1974 budget, two changes were made with Governor Carter's approval. One of these was to raise the organizational level at which decision packages were formulated—there would be fewer of these somewhat larger packages.[50]

The second change authorized by Governor Carter was that department-wide rankings for the larger agencies and departments would no longer be required. (Ranking requirements for smaller agencies were left unchanged.) This change was necessary, observed Minmier, because some agencies generated so many decision packages that "[t]he task of ranking these decision packages at both the division level and the agency level was stupendous."[51] The Georgia State Health Agency alone generated over 2100 decision packages in its two divisions with their seventeen major activities.

As a result of the change, departments and agencies were required to rank only those activities which made up each of the major "programs." (There were roughly 250 such programs listed in the 1974 budget.) But the time and effort involved in ranking at even this middle level was still excessive, particularly for the larger departments. As a result, "many departments failed to complete the [required] form."[52] So a further change was adopted for the FY 1975 budget: department-wide rankings were required for only "selected small departments," and all other departments were required to rank decision packages only at the activity level, the next step *below* the program level.

These activity level rankings were submitted to the OPB analysts who checked them for proper preparation and who then "selected those packages in each activity that they felt represented the 'base packages,' that is, those packages necessary to maintain the activity at its previous year's strength."[53] (The remaining decision packages were then submitted to the department head, along with the activity manager's ranking, for final ranking for the department.) In other words, the *previous year's* budget and activities became the keystone for budgetary decisions. Incrementalism was rediscovered.

As Minmier describes it, then, the continued difficulty of the process of ranking large numbers of decision packages led to a steady retreat from the objective of producing department-wide, much less government-wide, consolidated rankings.

Federal agencies also found it difficult to rank programs. In 1976 and 1977 the Environmental Protection Agency (EPA) conducted a "zerobase" review of a $96 million EPA-run "Interagency Energy/Environment Research and Development Program."[54] The EPA dutifully assembled the information into decision packages and then tried to rank the one hundred packages produced. Ranking presented some knotty problems. Managers found they could rank packages *within* each of the three major areas (health/ecological effects of energy development, pollution control technology, and program integration), but when funding increments within one of these three areas were compared with increments from another of the areas, "[e]xtreme difficulty was encountered." Such comparisons, in the EPA's euphemistic language, "were not vigorously produced." The EPA was troubled by its failure; its inability to rank all one hundred packages was seen as "not completely consistent with the spirit of ZBB." Nonetheless, due to the short time available and due to the more fundamental problem that the packages were "inherently very difficult to rank," the EPA officials felt they could not complete ZBB's requirements.[55]

Officials of NASA had similar problems, as this colloquy with Congressman Baucus at the NASA budget hearing demonstrates:

Mr. Baucus. It seems to me if we are going to make any decisions here as to what amounts to put in what programs, we need the benefit of your advice as to what programs are more important than others, and also what criteria you use to make your decisions. . . .

Dr. Fletcher. The problem, Mr. Baucus, is the difficulty in really measuring any science program. Not just NASA's, it is true of all science—NSF and others.

Mr. Baucus. It is true in all programs; it is true in the social programs as well. NASA is probably easier than most agencies. How do you measure HEW's programs. . . .

Dr. Fletcher. What we have to do then is to build systematically on past progress, planned accomplishments, and next-step requirements. We try to extrapolate that ahead several years and make a judgment as to what this particular science is going to contribute in the long run.

Mr. Baucus. How do you do that?

Dr. Fletcher. Take astronomy—

Mr. Baucus. Do you just throw darts at the wall, or just wake up one morning and say, this is what we will do? . . .

* * *

Mr. Baucus. What I am driving at is why is the Space Telescope so important now, today, compared to other alternatives you could pursue?

Dr. Fletcher. The Space Telescope should be compared with other science programs.

Mr. Baucus. I am trying to find out what criteria you used in making that judgment.

Dr. Fletcher. It is very difficult to balance off hospitals versus telescopes. The overall priorities are considered at OMB. Ultimately, the President decides what the priorities are and submits his budget to the Congress. We cannot balance off science versus applications by asking what are the long-term and short-term benefits, what are the long-term and short-term costs of each of those programs. The final decisions, at any level, are judgmental. The Space Telescope is probably the highest-priority science program right now, in the country.

Mr. Baucus. But why?[56]

Congressman Baucus never did get a satisfactory answer to his question.

Experiences with ranking by the other federal agencies during preparation of the FY 1979 budget were similarly mixed. Health, Education, and Welfare argued, reported *The Wall Street Journal*, that "it would be absurd to try to rank its multitude of disparate programs in strict order of priority."[57] After much discussion with OMB, HEW was allowed to rank only those 300 packages (out of a total of 1200) lying around the margin. After agreeing on what the minimums were, the Secretary and Undersecretary, according to a staff assistant, "spent the majority of their time concentrating on and manipulating the margins . . . "[58]

Just what the ranking process accomplished in the Public Health Service, one of HEW's constituent agencies, was unclear. A top budgeter in the PHS commented that "a great deal was learned about the overall priority of programs in PHS through ZBB." But what was the benefit of this knowledge? He goes on to state that:

> In some cases, programs which were believed all along to be of low priority in fact did show up as low priority when a formal ranking was done. Did this mean they were eliminated or reduced in the budget submission? In some cases, yes; in most cases, no.[59]

Commerce Secretary Kreps flatly refused to rank her Department's 406 separate decision packages. One Commerce official pointed out that Commerce was supposed to rank such disparate programs as the federal subsidy for merchant ship construction, aid to cities, fisheries research, fire prevention, and an agricultural census, and he explained that "the Secretary resisted doing this in so simplistic a fashion."[60] Another top Commerce administrator said in one interview that "Our Secretary is an economist who is not going to trade off apples and oranges . . . In a political environment, it [ranking] doesn't work that effectively."[61] In a second interview, this administrator also said that such ranking made no sense, and argued that, "[i]f they [the OMB] could tell us how it made sense, we would do it." This administrator went on to say that although OMB was "furious" at such forthright resistance, "We've taken the heat on it, and we've politely stood our ground."[62]

While Blandin and Donahue, the two OMB staffers writing in *The Bureaucrat*, felt that ranking was the ZBB requirement "most difficult to implement from a bureaucratic/political point of view",[63] several departments found a simple and ingenious solution to their own ranking problems. *The Wall Street Journal* reported that Department of Transportation officials "automatically gave existing programs the highest priorities and gave proposed new programs the lowest priorities."[64] The Department of Transportation was not alone in its decision to give current activities the highest priority. In his discussion of ZBB in the Department of Agriculture, one former Agriculture budgeter argues that, "There is no point in ranking programs at this stage [the drawing up of minimum level packages] since they share a common *high* priority."[65]

The budget director of ACTION admits that "minimum levels were generally proposed at close to the current services level, and not taken seriously."[66] In the Small Business Administration all minimum level packages were given the highest priority, while those below the OMB's funding guideline were almost entirely proposals for program improvements. Most current level and some improved level packages came somewhere in between, either just above or below the OMB guideline. Thus, said SBA officials, "we were not too concerned with our proposed rankings of minimum levels . . ." Instead, attention was given to the analysis of "most of the current levels and all the improved levels."[67]

Ranking of programs in the Department of Defense is a more complicated story. Each major component of the Department grouped its programs into three (and ultimately seven) "bands"—categories of relative importance. The categories went in ascending order of priority from improving ways of getting the job done to simply maintaining current force readiness. Only those programs in the two bands expected to be closest to the final margin—"i.e., encompassing the most likely range of final fiscal constraints"—were ranked item-by-item.[68] Then the staff of the Office of the Secretary of Defense prepared a DOD-wide ranking based on the bands, the component rankings, and staff recommendations. This ranking was used as the basis for the Secretary's discussions with the major components and for his final decisions.

Although from this account the ZBB process proved useful, an Air Force budgeter who helped develop the simplified procedures used by DOD suggested a number of further modifications which shed some doubt on the usefulness of the procedures. He recommends that the ranking of programs in decrements below the spending guideline base be discontinued ("The concept of taking things out of a budget, especially recently approved programs, can be a traumatic experience."). He further maintains that ranking each item within the broad bands is non-productive ("Incrementally addressing over one hundred separate items is a make-work exercise") and proposes to reduce greatly the number of decision units ("I believe we should give serious consideration to a single, or relatively few, service-oriented decision units . . ."). Overall, he would like the process "to focus on the margin" and not on the " 'no issue' base."[69]

Despite the fact that several departments failed to rank their packages in accordance with instructions, the OMB was not in any position to insist on absolute fidelity to ZBB procedures, for it refused to do any ranking of decision packages at all! "It would be unfair," said one

OMB ZBB expert to a *Wall Street Journal* reporter, to expect the OMB to do such rankings because that would amount to comparing apples and oranges. The *Journal's* reporter in turn observed, "This, of course, is what many department budget men thought when President Carter ordered them to cross-rank disparate programs within their departments in the first place." The reporter quoted one "disgusted" bureaucrat as saying "The whole system is ultimately a fraud—absolute nonsense—if OMB doesn't apply its own rules to itself." The result, this bureaucrat went on to say (as summarized by the reporter), was that President Carter's "final budget decisions will be made the same way other Presidents made them—by hunch and by seat-of-the-pants responses to powerful pressure groups. If so, what was the point of all the agonizing and paperwork at lower levels?"[70] One "old hand" at OMB commented that ZBB did enable an OMB budget examiner to tell the OMB Director which items could be cut without too much agency protest and which would be appealed to the President. But he also observed that, "A good examiner could always tell you that."[71]

Consolidating decision packages into a smaller number of broader rankings is the next stage in the process. Although the top managers are supposed to rely on consolidated rankings in making their final decisions, a key question arises: who are the consolidators? After all, it is a matter of great political consequence which programs get grouped with what other programs. If a program ranked number 5 is consolidated with a program ranked number 10, the former program's overall ranking goes down, while the latter's rises. Bureaus ranked high will thus want to stay aloof; those ranked low will want in. For some programs, central budget examiners may wish to follow a "divide and conquer" strategy; vulnerable agencies will try to use the counter-strategy of seeing that their programs are consolidated with those of less vulnerable agencies.[72] For other programs, roles (and therefore strategies) may be reversed.

Astute bureaucrats are well aware of these political possibilities. In their study of PPBS in federal recreation programs, Nienaber and Wildavsky found that the Forest Service objected to having its resource conservation programs (water, soil, scarce minerals) included under the program titled "Adequate Supply of Farm and Forest Products." The Forest Service feared that these "soft," relatively unquantifiable outputs would suffer when placed alongside the other "harder" production activities in the program, such as farm and forest products like crops and timber. Inclusion of the "soft" programs in a "Natural Resources Conservation" category was preferred.[73]

The consolidation process under ZBB left similar room for political considerations. The leaders of ACTION attempted with some success to get the OMB to compare their international programs (such as the Peace Corps) *not* with ACTION's domestic programs (such as VISTA) but with *other agencies'* international aid programs.[74] It is clear that ACTION's leaders thought their own international programs compared favorably with those of other agencies. As OMB staffers Blandin and Donahue summarize their own experiences with this matter, ". . . the increasing aggregation of decision packages was a source of some conflict."[75]

Information could also be hidden inside the consolidated rankings just as it could be hidden inside decision packages. One commentator on the Department of Defense effort noted:

> In Defense most decision units submitted to OSD [the Office of Secretary of Defense] are already highly aggregated. As a result it was in many cases extremely difficult to describe the content of a decision unit, not to mention the various packages within that unit.[76]

Several other federal participants also complained that valuable program information was buried in these hierarchical consolidations.[77]

Summarizing these various strategies, Suver and Brown comment that there seem to be numerous methods of beating the system; by putting items in decision packages reviewed and approved at lower levels, lower level managers can "hide inefficiencies, scratch each other's back, include expenses to buy off employees, or label featherbedding items as essential." "The result," the authors suggest, "may be that significant inefficiencies in an organization will not be revealed by this approach."[78]

Though Pyhrr and Cheek are aware of ZBB's vulnerability to such tactics, both think that managers can counteract them.[79] But to the extent that managers are overburdened with other duties and are forced to rely on summaries of the departmental rankings, which Pyhrr suggests will be the case,[80] then who provides the summaries becomes important. And of course, the most knowledgeable summarizers are the people in the agency which initiated the gamesmanship in the first place.

Evaluating the frequency and effectiveness of such ranking games is difficult. The games are often ones of concealment, after all.[81] But it should be noted that, according to Blandin and Donahue of the OMB, "Most [OMB budget] examiners believe that the agencies' ranking reflected a fair, meaningful, and candid portrayal of priorities."[82] Playing games, at least the more flagrant ones, are probably thought to be counterproductive in the long run. Straightforward and open arguments to top departmental officials and OMB examiners about a program's necessity and political popularity may be a much wiser strategy.

So far we have discussed two problems of ranking: the cognitive problems involved in not knowing how to rank, and the political problems involved in not wanting to rank and in manipulating the rankings. There is a third problem that is a mix of these two. It has to do with the fact that sometimes *separate* decision packages (whether in the same agency or in different agencies) are *interdependent*. NASA, for example, was bothered by this. In the budget hearings quoted earlier, the NASA Administrator repeatedly avoided requests to rank NASA programs, on the grounds that they often depended on each other. In terms of scientific discovery, the orbiting space telescope offered the greatest promise. But to launch the telescope into orbit, the Space Shuttle had to be operational. Similarly, the Kennedy Spaceflight Center in Florida, which launches NASA's satellites, consumes a substantial chunk of NASA's budget. But as the Center's Director described it at the budget hearings, his job was to launch what other NASA centers sent him. He felt he didn't have much choice in the matter: ". . . there aren't many decision package levels that I can see."[83]

The EPA was plagued by the same kind of problem. Referring to the "disparate yet interconnected" activities of the Energy/Environment R&D Program, the EPA Report cited the example of the development of an instrument to measure pollution concentrations in the environment, and the simultaneous development of control hardware to reduce the release of that pollutant. In some instances, the Report pointed out, the capabilities of the pollution control hardware "will dictate the performance specifications of the required [measurement] instrument." As a consequence, "the program managers found it exceedingly difficult to mold together the three major areas and to rank order the combined list of decision packages."[84] In the full-scale FY 1979 federal ZBB effort, problems of interdependence also plagued a number of other agencies. The Justice Department commented that its agencies "found that it was particularly difficult to fit crosscutting functions into the ZBB framework." Housing and Urban Development mentioned its difficulty ranking programs which were integrally involved with each other but which had different priorities. Draper and Pitsvada, who cite these and other examples, suggest that these problems with ZBB are of a "more structural nature."[85] But their solution to this problem with ranking mostly involves even more extensive ranking.[86] There are times when fighting fire with fire is an appropriate strategy, but we're not sure that this is one of those times.

There is a fourth kind of problem that ranking faces: it may be that many programs are in fact *equal* in importance with respect to political, economic, and other criteria. Assume that priorities are to be expressed in the form of a ZBB-style ranking. A program of less importance to an agency will have received less money over the years than a program of greater importance. But if the less important program remains worth doing at all within a given budget, it must be in "balance" in a rough sort of way with the seemingly more important program. Otherwise no money at all would be spent on it. So any budget increases must then be allocated *proportionally* to the two programs, with the more important agency getting the larger share. But the relative *significance* of the larger and smaller shares will be equal, and hence should be ranked at the same level. As economists put it, rational managers should allocate funds so that the marginal costs and marginal benefits of all programs are *equal*. But if the costs and benefits of our incremental decision packages are to be equal, this obviously means that such packages can't be ranked![87]

Although Peter Pyhrr addresses the difficulties of ranking numerous and non-comparable decision packages, his solutions do not resurrect ranking's role in zero-base budgeting. One of his solutions is simply only to rank packages around the cutoff line. This is what traditional budgeting does, in effect, all the time. A second solution is to not consolidate decision packages above a certain level in the organization. Major allocation decisions are thus made much as before. Phyrr's final remedy is to use a committee to do the ranking.[88] Each committee member rates each package on each (differentially weighted) criterion, and their scores are combined into one final score. Packages are then ranked on the basis of this score. But such committee voting may merely compound ignorance instead of pooling wisdom. In addition, such voting is extraordinarily sensitive to political manipulation. Who selects the members of this key committee? Who decides which weighting criteria are most important? In what sequence are issues brought up? Should Robert's Rules of Order apply? To solve such quandaries, Peter Pyhrr and his zero-base budgeting procedures offer us no guidance.

Adjusting Budgets to Changing Economic Conditions

One final question on ranking now bears examination: did the rankings produced in these governments and agencies provide a means of adjusting expenditures to changing economic conditions, by simply allowing budgeters to move the cutoff line up or down as conditions warranted? Pyhrr devoted the entire Chapter 6 of his book to a description of how organizations could use ZBB to adapt to such changing conditions.

Minmier's study in Georgia presents clear evidence on this issue, for he found that during Governor Carter's administration revenue conditions during budget formulation twice changed considerably, first for the better, and then for the worse. In neither case, Minmier found, was the process of changing departmental spending plans as effortless as Pyhrr's methods would suggest.

According to Minmier, during preparation of the 1974 fiscal year budget, very restrictive departmental budgetary guidelines were established. However, revenues higher than expected were generated by Georgia's expanding economy. But "[i]nstead of shifting the cutoff line downward to include more marginal decision packages, the Governor requested new decision packages from some of his departments to help him allocate additional funds."[89] In reaction to these fortuitously high revenues, the 1975 fiscal year planning was conducted without the use of departmental guidelines. Department heads submitted excessively large budgetary requests. When budget levels were reduced to more acceptable levels, the departments discovered that their priorities changed. Consequently, "many departments had to rank their decision packages again to reflect their priorities at the lower level of funding."[90] One departmental budget analyst quoted by Minmier put the problem succinctly:

> The priority ranking of our decision packages when we expect 140% funding simply is not the same as when we expect 115% funding.[91]

There are hints that during the lengthy preparation of the FY 1979 budget, some federal agencies experienced the same phenomenon. Partway through preparation of the Public Health Service budget, PHS budgeters were given a new budget target by the HEW Secretary that was some $400 million less than they had earlier been led to expect. One upshot was "further reranking . . ."[92] In the Small Business Administration, top administrators gave their program officials no target figure for their early ranking. When the OMB finally supplied the ceiling through its Presidential Policy Guidance Letter, the outlay ceiling proved lower than expected and, as an SBA budgeter put it, "This would have a significant effect on our final rankings."[93]

Such a reranking should come as no surprise. Economists call it "the income effect," and it is descriptive of how individuals behave in response to changing income levels. It is apparently also descriptive of

how managers in agencies behave. In the prototypical example beloved
by economists, if a person has been subsisting only on potatoes because that is all he can afford, and then his income goes up, he doesn't
generally continue buying only potatoes. Instead, he may start to buy
some meat. In fact, he may completely *stop* buying potatoes. His
"underlying" preferences may not have changed—he may always have
preferred meat to potatoes—but under different income levels, his preferences are simply *revealed* in different ways.

Such shifts in relative preferences don't *have* to occur. Preferences
may be such that spending on different goods remains in the same
proportions as income changes. Preferences are, after all, individual
matters. The point is that spending priorities *may* change as budgets
change, while underlying preferences remain the same, and there is
nothing irrational—or even political—about this happening. The problem which the income effect poses for ZBB is that the only way to
cope with it is to return the decision packages to their creators for
reformulation and reranking.[94] All previous efforts would thus be
wasted.

OMB's survey on the role of ZBB information of the FY 1979 budget
produced little criticism of the ranking procedures by the agencies.
Perhaps for some reason the "income effect" occurred only in isolated
instances. Analysts Draper and Pitsvada suggest two reasons why this
may have been the case. First, the agencies may have already had their
"mark"—their budget guideline—when they did their final ranking.
Second, perhaps the agencies "are more proficient at estimating their
upcoming 'mark' than most people realize." Draper and Pitsvada conclude that:

> Whatever the case, there still is no denying that ranking has to proceed
> within an environment where a "mark," if not yet established, is at least
> approximated. If a substantially different ceiling is later given an agency,
> then reranking would and should of course occur.[95]

In sum, it is fair to say that the ranking process makes unrealistic
demands on budgeters: too many decision packages are produced;
most packages have no common basis of comparison; and some packages are interdependent, and are thus even more difficult to rank. The
"income effect," moreover, makes ranking highly uncertain in the absence of spending guidelines, while spending guidelines vitiate the zero-
base character of the ZBB process. In consequence, most rankings—
among minimums, for example—are almost completely ignored by top
decision makers. Inevitably the process gets simplified, in fact if not

in name. Minimums are no longer ranked; only those packages falling around the funding guidelines are prioritized. Even the packages from different agencies falling around the guidelines are seldom ranked against each other, and the higher one ascends in the bureaucracy, the less ranking is carried on.[96] In Georgia, over several years' time, ranking requirements were successively relaxed. In one year with the federal government, very few complete rankings were made. Time will tell if ranking practices in coming years will be similarly loosened.

A Flaw in the Logic of ZBB

As if the unsolved intellectual and political problems of ranking large numbers of decision packages were not enough, we would like to close this section by pointing out a purely *logical* flaw in ZBB's procedures. The success of ZBB depends on the assumption that *if* decision packages are ranked and decisions are made through the imposition of a cutoff line, *then* optimal decisions will result. In fact, this deduction is not always valid. In their 1961 book on the problem of military budgeting, Hitch and McKean considered the use of priority listings (rankings) as a way of making budgetary decisions. But they point out that in budgeting, the problem is one of *allocation*, and not a settling of priorities. After a careful discussion of the possible uses of listings, they conclude that use of the listings "does not solve the allocation problem and can even trap us into adopting foolish policies."[97]

Imagine four decision packages. The first package contains 70 units of benefits. The cost of the package is $40. The benefit/cost ratio is therefore 1.75. The second package has a value of 51 and a cost of $30; the b/c ratio is 1.7. The third package has a value of 32 and a cost of $20; the b/c ratio is 1.6. The fourth package has a value of 11 and costs of $10, with a b/c ratio of 1.1. If we wished to rank the packages by their benefit/cost ratios, we would produce Table 1.

Table 1

Decison Package	Benefits	Costs	Benefits/Costs
1	70 units	$40	1.75
2	51 units	$30	1.7
3	32 units	$20	1.6
4	11 units	$10	1.1

Now let us follow ZBB's procedures to decide which decision packages to adopt. If our budget is $60, the optimal solution is to fund packages 1 and 3. We would reach this decision by first picking 1, since it has the highest b/c ratio. Because 1 costs $40 and our budget is $60, we are left with $20. The next "best" package is 2, but it is too expensive at $30. So we skip over it and select 3, which we can afford at $20. The ZBB decision rules work fine at this budget level: we have spent the budget and received 102 units of benefits. So far so good.

But look what happens if our budget is $50. If we follow the ZBB decision rule, we would first pick 1 as before and get 70 units of benefits. We then have $10 left over, and the only other package we can afford is 4 at $10. We thus accumulate 81 units of benefits. But if we *skip* package 1 and fund both 2 and 3 instead, we will have spent our whole budget, and we will have received 83 units of benefits from the two chosen packages, better than the 81 units from package 1 and 4. We are better off if we *don't* follow ZBB procedures![98]

What this means is that even if we all agree on the data and the measures to be used, there is no guarantee that moving down the list of packages will produce the optimal choice, when the packages are ranked in terms of their benefit/cost ratios. In fact, *any* ranking scheme will suffer from the same problem. If, for example, we somehow come up with a ranking of the packages that puts them in the 2-3-1-4 order, which optimally solves the $50 budget constraint, we find that it flunks the *$40* budget constraint test. In this latter case, ZBB procedures would have us pick package 2 (51 units of benefit, $30 cost) plus package 4 (11 units of benefit, $10 cost) for a total benefit of 62 units, whereas if we picked 1 at a $40 cost, we find ourselves with 70 units of benefits. We are again worse off with ZBB.[99] On occasion, things *may* work out just fine, *but not* necessarily.[100]

Affecting the likelihood of the "knapsack problem" actually occurring is the overall size of the decision packages relative to the agency's entire budget. With "large" packages, an agency is likely to run into the problem; the creation of "small" decision packages is one way of avoiding it. There is some evidence of this occurring in the National Science Foundation's preparation of its FY 1979 budget under ZBB. Draper and Pitsvada report that the decision packages produced by the NSF were fairly large in comparison to its overall budget. Ranking of the incremental packages quickly brought the NSF up against the OMB's expenditure guideline, leaving the NSF very unhappy that some programs wouldn't receive increases. In consequence, the NSF felt compelled to retrace its steps and reconstruct the decision packages, say Draper and Pitsvada, "so as to spread smaller increases to many areas rather than large increases to few areas."[101] It is not certain, but on the face of it, the "knapsack problem" would appear to have been involved. And apparently the NSF was not the only agency to have engaged in this kind of behavior.[102]

The ranking process, it seems, has even more severe problems than first meet the eye. The economist Jack Hirshleifer summarizes the matter nicely:

> Unfortunately, it is *not* in general true that investment opportunities can be uniquely ranked; the desirability of any one may be affected by the other project elements in any over-all package into which it enters. Thus, a correct ranking rule for individual projects is not generally possible.[103]

What more need be said in conclusion about the ranking process? People can't do it very well in practice, and in theory it suffers from a fatal flaw.

Notes

1. Logan M. Cheek, *Zero-Base Budgeting Comes of Age* (New York: The American Management Association, 1977).
2. Logan M. Cheek, *Zero Base Budgeting Comes Of Age*, p. 46, emphasis in original.
3. "The Zero-Base Approach To Government Budgeting," *Public Administration Review* 37 (January/February 1977), p. 3, emphasis added.
4. See Section 6c, p. 22343.
5. Most other articles surveyed did not go into this level of detail on decision-package formulation and hence avoided the issue entirely.
6. Pyhrr, *Zero-Base Budgeting*, pp. 10-14. Paul J. Stonich, in his *Zero-Base Planning and Budgeting* (Homewood, Ill.: Dow Jones-Irwin, 1977) likewise comments: "To analyze the operation effectively, the lower level manager requires planning assumptions about inflation rates and salary increases the same as a manager preparing a traditional budget. In addition to these economic and planning assumptions, the lower level manager requires information about service-level requirements for allied departments. The more complete the assumptions and plans, the easier it is for the manager to prepare his budget." (p. 20).
7. For an example of where they were once *not* used in Georgia, see our subsection titled "Adjusting Budgets to Changing Economic Conditions" later in this Chapter. That particular experience showed how necessary they are.
8. P. 22342.
9. Of course, if we knew this for all our activities, we would have far less trouble with many of ZBB's other procedures, but then we wouldn't need ZBB at all, because *performance budgeting* would have succeeded thirty years ago.
10. That the ZBB literature does not recognize this problem may account for some of the difficulties bureaucrats have in implementing the concept.

11. Roy Lee Hogan, "Zero-Base Budgeting: A Rationalistic Attempt to Improve the Texas Budget System," (University of Texas, Austin, December 1975). Hogan's study was based primarily on the experiences of three agencies with ZBB—the Department of Public Health, the Department of Public Safety and the Department of Corrections.
12. Page 292 of Compendium.
13. Ibid, emphasis in original.
14. Ibid, p. 294.
15. Ibid, p. 295.
16. Ibid, p. 296.
17. See John D. LaFaver, "Zero-Base Budgeting in New Mexico," *State Government* 47 (Spring 1974).
18. Ibid, p. 111.
19. Minmier, *An Evaluation of the Zero-Base Budgeting System in Governmental Institutions*, p. 173.
20. Ibid.
21. Ibid.
22. For more recent evidence of the troubles that Georgia budgeters have with the concept of the "minimum," see Thomas P. Lauth, "Zero-Base Budgeting in Georgia State Government: Myth and Reality," *Public Administration Review* 38 (September/October 1978), especially pp. 422-423.
23. The Subcommittee had requested that NASA do an experimental "zero-based" analysis on the Research and Program Development portion of its budget. A special day was set aside by the Subcommittee just to review the results of the experiment. The Consumer Product Safety Commission and the Environmental Protection Agency ran similar experiments at the same time.
24. U.S. House of Representatives, Hearings Before the Subcommittee of the Committee on Appropriations, "Part 5: National Aeronautics and Space Administration," 95th Congress, First Session, March 29-30, 1977 (Washington D.C.: U.S. Government Printing Office, 1977) pp. 981, 982.
25. Nanette Blandin and Arnold Donahue, "ZBB: Not A Panacea, But A Definite Plus—An OMB Perspective," *The Bureaucrat* 7 (Spring 1978), p. 53.
26. There probably are "natural" minimums for some tasks, such as in "lumpy" capital investment projects. One ought not build a bridge three-quarters of the way across a river, for example, and sending a man to the moon probably also requires a certain "minimum" expenditure. Most government programs are not very lumpy, however. They are generally rather divisible. (Figure 1 is a production function for a divisible program.)
27. Hogan comments that advocating the use of arbitrary fixed-percentage minimums "would be an admission that there is no validity in the identification of minimum levels." See page 311 in *Compendium*.
28. Pyhrr, *Zero-Base Budgeting*, p. 86.
29. "Zero Base Budgeting in the States," (1976), in *Compendium*.
30. Frank D. Draper and Bernard T. Pitsvada, *A First Year Assessment of Zero-Base Budgeting in the Federal Government—Another View* (Arlington, Virginia: The Association of Government Accountants, 1978), p. 30.
31. Ibid, pp. 26-27.

32. Herbert Mills, "Zero-base Budgeting: The Initial Experience in SBA," *The Bureaucrat* 7 (Spring 1978), p. 29.

33. Quoted by Joel Havemann in "The Tale of How One Agency Used ZBB— And Lived To Tell About It," *National Journal* 10 (18 February 1978), p. 268.

34. Tony Itteilag, "FY 1979 ZBB Formulation in the Public Health Service," *The Bureaucrat* 7 (Spring 1978), p. 21.

35. Although we have no evidence on this, there is a hint that such an incentive appears in the ranking process to be discussed later in the Chapter. A commentator on ZBB in the Department of Defense noted that some participants saw explicit priority rankings as a "kamikaze" process in which one department's lower rankings might serve to finance other departments' higher priorities. See John R. Quetsch, "ZBB and DoD," *The Bureaucrat* 7 (Spring 1978), p. 33. We would be surprised if this incentive doesn't exist in the formulation of minimums.

36. Minmier, pp. 173-176.

37. Allen Schick, "Zero Base Budgeting and Sunset: Redundancy or Symbiosis?" *The Bureaucrat* 6 (Spring 1977), p. 18.

38. Page 289 in *Compendium*.

39. Ibid, p. 289.

40. Ibid, p. 290.

41. The beekeepers and the fire fighting examples are cited in *National Journal* 8 (22 May 1976), p. 707. Pyhrr, *Zero-Base Budgeting*, pp. 39-45 and Carter, *Why Not The Best?* pp. 129-130, cite the Highway Patrol example and Carter cites the grass mowing example (pp. 128-129).

42. We are normally not this suspicious, but Pyhrr and Carter seem to contradict each other on the Highway Patrol example. Pyhrr ascribes the change to ZBB in *Zero-Base Budgeting*, pp. 39-45. Carter in *Why Not the Best?*, pp. 129-130, ascribes the change to a constitutional amendment which he supported authorizing the payment of monetary rewards to state employees who suggest ways of cutting state costs. For those suggestions adopted the employee can be awarded ten percent of the money saved by the state in the first year.

43. The selection of alternatives to make some preferred option look good is known in some circles as the "sandwich strategy" and in other circles as the "Option B" effect. Whatever it is called, it is an old political ploy well-suited to use in ZBB.

44. Schick and Keith, in *Compendium*, p. 23.

45. "ZBB: No Panacea," *The Bureaucrat* 7 (Spring 1978), p. 54.

46. Itteilag, "FY 1979 Formulation in the Public Health Service," pp. 20, 21.

47. Draper and Pitsvada, *A First Year Assessment*, p. 46.

48. Ibid, p. 47.

49. Minmier, *An Evaluation of the Zero-Base Budgeting System in Governmental Institutions*, p. 76.

50. It was recognized, says Minmier, "that a certain degree of detailed information would be omitted" through preparation of these less detailed decision packages, but there was a "general consensus of the budget analysts that the expected improvements in information flows would justify such a sacrifice." See page 79.

51. Minmier, p. 80.
52. Ibid, p. 105.
53. Ibid.
54. The Senate Appropriations Committee asked the Congressional Budget Office (CBO) to review this program. The CBO turned to the EPA to assemble the information in the ZBB format. (See U.S. Congress, Congressional Budget Office, "An Experiment in Zero-Base Budget Analysis—Fiscal Year 1978," Interagency Energy/Environment R&D Program Report, March 1977). The CBO was overseeing similar efforts by the National Aeronautics and Space Administration and the Consumer Product Safety Commission at the same time. Due to the short period of time that the agencies were given for the review, these ZBB exercises can't be considered definitive evidence as to how ZBB works. The agencies' experiences are nonetheless instructive.
55. All comments are from the CBO, "An Experiment . . . ," p. 15.
56. U.S. House of Representatives, Appropriations Hearings, 1977, NASA, pp. 50-51.
57. Dennis Farney, "Birth Pains: Zero-Base Budgeting, A Pet Carter Project, Is Off To A Slow Start," The Wall Street Journal, December 19, 1977, p. 22.
58. Thomas De Hanas, "Zero-base Budgeting and the Management Review Process in the Department of Health, Education and Welfare," The Bureaucrat, 7 (Spring 1978), p. 25.
59. Tony Itteilag, "FY 1979 ZBB Formulation in the Public Health Service," p. 20.
60. Edward Cowan, "Zero-Base Budgeting: It Made A Difference," The New York Times, January 22, 1978, Section 3, p. 14. Despite the title of this article, virtually all its evidence demonstrates that ZBB made very little difference at all.
61. William J. Eaton (Knight News Service), "Zero-Base Budgeting—Some Say It's Nothing," San Francisco Sunday Examiner-Chronicle, January 15, 1978, Section C, p. 13.
62. Edward Cowan, "Zero-Base Budgeting," p. 14.
63. "ZBB: Not A Panacea," p. 54.
64. Dennis Farney, "Birth Pains," p. 22.
65. Jerome A. Miles, "Fundamentals of Budgeting and ZBB," The Bureaucrat 7 (Spring 1978), p. 44, emphasis added.
66. Emerson Markham, "Zero-base Budgeting in ACTION," p. 49.
67. Herbert T. Mills, "Zero-base Budgeting: The Initial Experience in SBA," The Bureaucrat 7 (Spring 1978), p. 29.
68. John R. Quetsch, "ZBB and DoD," p. 34.
69. Hans H. Driessnack, "Zero-base Budgeting: Our First Year," The Bureaucrat 7 (Spring 1978), p. 40.
70. Dennis Farney, "Birth Pains," p. 22.
71. Cowan, "Zero-Base Budgeting," p. 14.
72. Congress occasionally uses this counter-strategy against the President by grouping programs it wants—but he doesn't—in the same bill along with the programs he does want. The President is left in a "take it or leave it" position.

73. See *The Budgeting and Evaluation of Federal Recreation Programs*, pp. 122-123.
74. Emerson Markham, "Zero-base Budgeting in ACTION," p. 49.
75. "ZBB: Not A Panacea," p. 54.
76. Quetsch, "ZBB and DoD," p. 34.
77. See Richard E. Miller, "ZBB in the Federal Government: Some Current Impressions," *The Bureaucrat* 7 (Spring 1978), p. 8.
78. George Suver and Ray Brown, "Where Does Zero-Base Budgeting Work?" *Harvard Business Review* 55 (November-December 1977), p. 81.
79. Pyhrr, for example, says in a 1977 article that: "If done properly, the zero-base approach is not subject to the gamesmanship one might anticipate." See his "The Zero-Base Approach to Government Budgeting," p. 8. Cheek claims that "Nothing in zero-base budgeting will substitute for informed review by higher-level management. With that informed review, however, playing such games is extremely difficult." See *Zero-Base Budgeting Comes of Age*, p. 159.
80. In "The Zero-Base Approach to Government Budgeting," p. 7, he admits that in large organizations "top management may be forced to rely primarily on management summaries in lieu of concentrating on the decision packages." The same problem was touched on in his *Zero-Base Budgeting*, pp. 96ff.
81. For an amusing tale of one such game, see James Q. Wilson, "Zero-Base Budgeting Comes To Washington," *The Alternative: An American Skeptic*, February 1977, p. 5.
82. "ZBB: Not A Panacea," p. 54.
83. U.S. House of Representatives, Appropriations Hearings, 1977, NASA, p. 978. Similar complaints were voiced in New Jersey: "Some agencies complained that their program activities are so interrelated that one activity cannot be separated for funding purposes without affecting several other program activities." See Scheiring, "Zero-Based Budgeting in New Jersey," p. 376 in Compendium.
84. U.S. Congress, Congressional Budget Office, "An Experiment in Zero-Base Budget Analysis," p. 15.
85. Draper and Pitsvada, *A First Year Assessment*, p. 36.
86. Ibid, pp. 84-5.
87. This is not an assertion that the *total* benefits and costs of all programs are equal; they may well not be. The point is that if managers have been allocating funds rationally the *next* dollar to be allocated would provide equal benefits in *all* programs. (Even this is a bit of a simplification. See the Appendix for a more technically accurate description of the problem.)
88. See Pyhrr, "Zero-Base Budgeting," pp. 116-117 and *Zero-Base Budgeting*, pp. 89-92.
89. Minmier, *An Evaluation*, p. 169.
90. Ibid, p. 153. In light of Minmier's statement that budget requests "much in excess" of what could be funded were submitted, it is amusing to recall Governor Carter's complaint about such requests in his first weeks as Governor: "Following the election, I began to prepare the budget for the coming year. Piled on a table were departmental funding requests that amounted to more than half again as much money as would be available.

No one had made any attempt to assess the worth of the requests or to arrange them in any sort of priority. I worked with my budget staff every night for six weeks on this confusing mess, and I became more convinced than ever that my own developing concepts of what I called 'zero-base budgeting' were necessary." See pp. 126-127 of *Why Not The Best?*
91. Minmier, p. 169.
92. Itteilag, "FY 1979 ZBB Formulation," p. 19.
93. Herbert T. Mills, "Zero-base Budgeting," p. 28.
94. Of course, it would be possible ahead of time to have each agency formulate a whole set of packages and each department to rank them *for every possible budget*, but this would make a difficult job many times harder.
95. Draper and Pitsvada, *A First Year Assessment*, p. 60.
96. It is our suspicion that the departments and agencies which did make relatively complete rankings were either quite small and homogeneous (and thus packages were relatively comparable) or else were agencies (like the EPA) which had received relatively generous spending guidelines from the OMB. Particularly under the latter circumstance, ranking would be easier precisely because it meant less.
97. See Charles Hitch and Roland McKean, *The Economics of Defense in the Nuclear Age* (Cambridge, Mass.: Harvard University Press, 1961), p. 123. We thank Jon Bendor for pointing this discussion out to us.
98. In the literature of operations research, this is known as "the knapsack problem." Our example is adapted from one presented by Donald P. Gaver and Gerald L. Thompson in *Programming and Probability Models in Operations Research* (Monterey, California: Brooks/Cole Publishing Co., 1973), pp. 228-229.
99. Ironically, a "pure" form of ZBB would give the "optimal" result, if by this "pure" form we mean a global calculation of all possible combinations of decision packages. Thus ZBB's real-world procedures, our focus here, are a hindrance to the spirit of ZBB! Of course, since such global calculations are generally infeasible to carry out, this point is of purely theoretical interest.
100. Even if, by good fortune, we have stumbled into an optimal decision, but then the budget changes on us (as happened twice in four years in Georgia), we would have to send the decision packages back to the agencies for reranking. This effect is logically distinct from "the income effect," although the net result is the same: the packages have to be redone.
101. Draper and Pitsvada, *A First Year Assessment*, p. 49.
102. For a discussion of this problem, see Draper and Pitsvada's "Zero-Base Budgeting in the Federal Government; Some Preliminary Observations on the First Year's Effort," *The Government Accountants Journal* 27 (Spring 1978), p. 26.
103. Jack Hirshleifer, *Investment, Interest and Capital* (Englewood Cliffs, N.J.: Prentice-Hall, 1970), p. 47, emphasis in original.

Chapter 4

Does ZBB Reallocate Resources?

That ZBB shows us how to reallocate resources from less to more productive activities is the most important claim made for ZBB. When Peter Pyhrr cites twelve benefits of ZBB, for example, the first four concern reallocations.[1]

The best evidence on reallocations is in Minmier's study of Georgia, and Minmier does argue that ". . . there has been a substantial reallocation of financial resources within state government during Governor Carter's administration—especially during his first year in office."[2] The question is whether ZBB had anything to do with it. Budgeters in Georgia were still trying to figure out how to make ZBB work during Carter's first year in office.

All the evidence suggests that ZBB played a negligible role. From the questionnaire responses of the departmental budget analysts, Minmier concludes:

> The responses of the seventeen budget analysts present during the original implementation of zero-base budgeting were unanimous in expressing the opinion that there had been no apparent shifting of financial resources as a result of employing the zero-base budgeting system.[3]

From personal interviews with thirteen department heads, a similar conclusion is drawn:

> Two of the thirteen (15%) expressed the opinion that there may have been some reallocation of financial resources. . . . However, they were unable to give a single instance where the new budgeting system had reallocated resources in their own departments. The other eleven department heads (85%) indicated there had been no apparent reallocation of financial resources in their departments as a result of implementing zero-base budgeting.[4]

Governor Carter himself told Minmier in a January 1974 interview that, in Minmier's words, "it was the Executive Reorganization Act of 1972 that was the primary force in reallocating financial resources within the state of Georgia." He did assert, however, that it was *ZBB* which detected the "need" for consolidating similar governmental functions.[5] But given the great uncertainties and confusions accompanying the first year of ZBB in Georgia—with the production of "unknown" but "enormous" numbers of decision packages, as Minmier put it, and their wholesale return by the budget office for revisions by the departments—it is very unlikely that ZBB had much of an input into the reorganization effort. The Carter reorganization bill, after all, was submitted to the Legislature at the same time as the first Carter ZBB budget.

A final piece of evidence comes from Minmier's own examination of the 1972, 1973, and 1974 executive budgets. Could changes in the allocation of financial resources noticeable in these budgets be attributed to ZBB? Apparently not: ". . . it was impossible to correlate any such changes directly to the use of zero-base budgeting." Summing up his findings, Minmier concludes:

> [T]he zero-base budgeting system has not made a direct contribution to the reallocation of the state's financial resources. Throughout this investigation, there has not been a single verifiable instance where the new budgeting system has caused a shifting of financial resources other than during reorganization.[6]

Other investigations of the impact of ZBB on the Georgia budget have come to the same conclusions.[7]

What is the evidence for reallocation in other governments? Hogan's study of Texas does not address this issue at all. LaFaver's useful little account of a legislatively-based ZBB effort in New Mexico from 1970 through 1973 touches on something like "reallocation" of resources only in the first year of the effort. Ten agencies (whose appropriations constituted about one percent of the total state general fund appropriations) were requested to justify their programs and budget requests as though for the first time.[8] The Legislative Finance Committee which was running the ZBB experiment recommended that three of the ten agencies be abolished, and that the programs of two others be "substantially restructured." The other five agencies were left substantially unchanged. But it is difficult to know what to make of these examples, for LaFaver also tells us that "[t]he agencies were not selected randomly. Those chosen were generally controversial and thought to be in need of thorough scrutiny."[9] Did ZBB procedures produce these results? It sounds like the legislature intended to scrutinize these agencies, ZBB or no ZBB. LaFaver does note, for instance, that other agencies which did not undergo a formal ZBB review *also* had their operations re-structured and their budgets cut. There is nothing new in a legislative committee making life hard for some agencies. The use of ZBB in New Mexico may simply have been the *consequence*, rather than the *cause*, of an aggressive legislative committee and staff.

Scheiring's study of ZBB in New Jersey from 1974 to 1976 under Governor Brendan Byrne presents at best equivocal evidence on the role of ZBB in reallocations or cost-cutting. Scheiring points out that the state budget had grown at an average annual increase of 14.7 percent, and that Governor Byrne using ZBB had submitted only a 1.8 percent increase request for FY 1976. But Scheiring did not view the slower growth rate as evidence that ZBB had changed budgeting in New Jersey. He argues instead that without other factors, in particular "fiscal necessity," New Jersey could not have slowed down its budget growth so dramatically. He even states flatly that, "[n]o discernible benefits in cost reduction or management improvement resulted from the zero-base process."[10]

The account of ZBB's first year in Wilmington, Delaware by Singleton et al.[11] offers virtually no evidence of resource reallocation. Only two new or expanded "service levels" out of 196 decision packages were included above the cutoff point, though there were some cuts in other current services; no employees were laid off. Given Wilmington's revenues and its other fiscal problems, and given that tax increases were ruled out for "policy reasons," cuts in services were inevitable.[12] This is not an uncommon occurrence. All we know from this account is that cuts were made in low priority services. It is not unlikely that these same services would have been cut using Wilmington's previous budgetary methods.

On the federal level of government, it is difficult to tell whether ZBB has had any effect on the reallocation of resources from less productive programs to more productive ones. What evidence there is, however, suggests that not much reallocation has taken place. In the OMB's own survey, only six agencies reported that they had made some savings. Draper and Pitsvada's analysis of the OMB data suggested that "The sum total of these savings is a relatively small amount even if the agencies are given the benefit of every doubt." They also noted that four of the agencies reporting savings had received significant, "double digit" increases in their budgets anyway. They conclude that "As it was conducted, the FY 1979 budget preparation demonstrated that

ZBB will not result in large scale reallocation of resources within the government."[13] In similar fashion Richard Miller, writing in *The Bureaucrat*, concludes:

> In fact, there seems to be no evidence that any notable budgetary savings have been effected to this point as a result of the ZBB effort—except by accident.[14]

And after noting that every major federal program "is funded at or slightly above its current service level," Allen Schick concludes that ZBB has "changed the terminology of budgeting, but little more."[15]

Comments from some of the agencies are instructive. One top budgeter at HEW asserted to a *New York Times* reporter that ZBB "forces you to think through your priorities," but when asked by the reporter if this had made a difference in his department's ultimate budget choices, conceded that "I don't think they came out much differently." A Department of Defense budget official praised the involvement of lower-level, grass roots personnel in the budgetary process, but as to whether this had made any difference to his budget, he said, "Intuition tells me there was probably a different budget mix, but you can't put your finger on it."[16] In the Consumer Products Safety Commission, the comptroller stated that "I do not think that anyone really feels that ZBB is a special process that will reduce budgets or reorder priorities."[17]

There are, to be sure, several accounts of ZBB "successes." Upon closer examination, these successes turn out to be attributable not to ZBB but to the fact that President Carter's appointees have different concerns from their Republican predecessors. At the Commerce Department, for example, it was said that the "start-from-scratch" look showed that the National Bureau of Standards was in danger of becoming a second-rate scientific institution. On the basis of its importance to industry, Secretary Kreps sought and won $10 million from the OMB for a five-year program to restore the NBS' eminence.[18] But the decline of the NBS had been a matter of concern to the scientific and technical community for a number of years, and in 1977 *Science* magazine devoted a feature story to its problems.[19] Secretary Kreps and the OMB—and not ZBB—are to be credited with being the saviour of the National Bureau of Standards.

The Environmental Protection Agency, where ZBB was applied "with apparently dazzling results,"[20] is said to be another success story. According to the *National Journal*, by using ZBB the EPA was better able to coordinate its various pollution control programs: it was able to "cut through its organizational barriers and achieve coherent planning."[21] Even the OMB was reported to have been quite happy with EPA's performance.[22] As the tale is told,[23] top EPA officials toiled three weeks while closeted in a windowless conference room, setting the EPA budgetary priorities according to ZBB procedures. Several important decisions were made during this time. For instance, it was decided to concentrate on screening the nation's drinking water for cancer-causing chemicals, instead of increasing the control of industrial waste disposal practices. One administrator said that ZBB allowed the EPA to decide that the safety of public drinking water systems was more pressing; it wasn't that the waste disposal program was unimportant, he explained, but that the EPA probably couldn't afford it.[24] A second decision was to seek a substantial increase in funds for enforcement of the toxic substances control program in order to stop the marketing of dangerous chemicals before they do harm.[25] A third decision was to de-emphasize the noise pollution control program. The director of this program complained that without zero-based budgeting, his program would have gained rather than lost funds.[26] "This was a direct result of ZBB," agreed an EPA assistant administrator. "The public is very supportive of the program and we all have an aversion to noise here at EPA, but the people and resources for new priorities have to come from somewhere. As far as we know, very few people are being killed right now because of noise."[27]

However reasonable or desirable these decisions may have been, it is probable that many of the same decisions would have been made in the absence of zero-base budgeting. In 1974 Congress passed the Safe Drinking Water Act (P.L.93-523) in response to revelations by an environmental group, the Environmental Defense Fund, and the EPA that drinking water in the New Orleans area contained cancer-causing chemicals. In the years following passage of the Act, the EDF grew quite critical of the EPA and the Ford Administration for their lack of action in implementing the law. President Carter is more environmentally minded than his predecessor, and his OMB granted the EPA an increase in the program's employees from 334 to 500; when the EPA appealed for seventy-six more, it got fifty-five of them. This all occurred despite the fact that the EPA complained afterward that the OMB had reviewed the EPA budget in the same old way, too often substituting its judgment in setting budgetary priorities for that of the EPA.[28] We can thus surmise that the key variable affecting the EPA's success in increasing the program's budget was not ZBB—which the EPA felt that the OMB had ignored anyway—but the greater environmental concerns of the President and his budget officials.

Regarding the control of toxic substances, it wasn't until 1976 that

Congress even gave EPA the authority, in the Toxic Substances Control Act (P.L.94-469), to tackle this massive and enormously complex problem.[29] High rates of growth in this new program are thus to be expected for some time, particularly during the Carter Administration, and one doesn't need ZBB to know this.

Regarding the "new" go-slow approach to noise pollution control, this appears in fact to be a continuation of *old* priorities. The General Accounting Office criticized the EPA in 1977 for spending too little on noise control, and the program's director referred to his own program in a 1977 memo as one "whose statutory mandate has never been adequately funded and where the agency has received severe criticism for its previous performance."[30] In other words, noise pollution has for quite some time been a low EPA priority; its low priority in the Carter Administration unmistakably resembles its low priority in the Ford Administration. ZBB has not added anything new here either.

Contributing to the EPA's ability to comply with ZBB procedural requirements more easily than other agencies was the fact that $4.5 billion in sewer construction grants, some eighty percent of EPA's budget, was excluded from the zero-base procedures. Of equally great importance was the Carter Administration's willingness to increase the EPA budget by some twelve percent, compared to an increase of only some eight percent for the government as a whole.[31] Ranking and priority setting are always easier when resources are growing as rapidly as this. At any rate, the EPA ranked only the programs in the top ten percent of its budget, its director of program analysis saying, "That's all that's meaningful."[32] And since *The Wall Street Journal* described the EPA's decision-making process as "haggling and horsetrading," we can only take this to mean that the EPA budget was put together much as budgets are always put together.[33] In sum, this is not an impressive body of evidence on the ability of ZBB to reallocate resources.[34]

Involvement of Managers in the Budgetary Process

The final important claim that we will consider is that under ZBB managers become more involved in the budgetary process. The weight of evidence *does* support *this* claim. In Georgia, according to Minmier, seven of seventeen departmental budget analysts present at ZBB implementation reported their department heads to have become more involved in budgeting; ten of the analysts reported their departments' "first-line supervisors" also to have grown more involved. And fourteen of these same seventeen analysts reported that in general budget preparation took either much greater time (eight analysts) or slightly more time (six analysts).[35]

Of the other accounts of ZBB implementation in the states and cities—Hogan on Texas, Singleton et al. on Wilmington, possibly Scheiring on New Jersey—some evidence supports the claim, and none contradicts it. In the federal government greater involvement of top staff and political appointees was also typical. Draper and Pitsvada report that more than two-thirds of the agencies answering the OMB's survey indicated greater program manager involvement.[36]

But any new budget procedure takes more time and effort and involves officials in work they do not normally perform. The important question is whether this added involvement has any lasting benefits. Greater involvement by itself means little, and may indicate costly and inefficient budgeting if the outcomes are not correspondingly improved.[37] In other words, for managers not to be deeply involved in the budget process may be a wise use of their time. There may be more important things for them to do than to spend it on a process that they won't change much through their deep involvement. If the "much greater insight into the functions of State Government"[38] gained through such involvement in the budget process was *useful* to top executives, we would expect them to seek such insights even under incremental budgeting. But they apparently don't.[39] Either these executives are irrational, *or they know something*. Perhaps they know that deep insights into all sorts of governmental matters are very nice, but if they are of little help on the job, there is little reason to pursue them.

ZBB's Expected Benefits Don't Materialize—
But Some Unexpected Ones Do

ZBB does not produce on its claims. Yet a considerable number of participants in and observers of the process judge it to be a worthwhile activity. Why? Perhaps it generates some indirect benefits not anticipated by its creators.

This was the case with the Department of Agriculture's ZBB experiment in the early 1960s.[40] Wildavsky and Hammann's interviews uncovered a variety of reasons why many Agriculture officials professed to find ZBB useful, despite the fact that hardly anything in their budget had been changed. Four reasons in particular stood out: they felt reassured that they were acting "rationally", they believed that they learned something useful from the experience, they believed that 'somebody else' learned something useful, and some found ZBB to be politically useful.

For those who expressed positive feelings about ZBB, observed Wildavsky and Hammann, "the experience appears to have satisfied a longing to believe that they were proceeding according to the canons of rational methods of calculation."[41] To so believe would relieve the strain of believing in comprehensive, "rational" budgeting while practicing incremental and sequential budgeting. The experience also made some practitioners feel more important and useful. Budget officers in particular liked the attention budgeting was getting. Their activities were seen as more important, and they liked the fact that the Secretary of Agriculture himself attended departmental budget hearings.[42] No information in the more recent accounts of ZBB in action speaks to these points. But it is a remarkably prevalent theme in the "how to do it" ZBB literature. Logan Cheek, for example, in discussing organizations which have adopted ZBB, says that:

> [E]ven if they cannot quantify the benefits of zero-base budgeting (and most can), virtually all agree that their *comfort* over the quality of their decisions as well as their ability to develop responsible and responsive budgets has improved substantially.[43]

Given that the bulk of evidence on ZBB in Georgia and elsewhere suggests that ZBB had little effect on final outcomes, we suspect that this very lack of change may have proved reassuring to budgeters. Since they had been making the "right" decisions all along, and were now doing so with ZBB's rational-looking procedures, things couldn't have been better.

Wildavsky and Hammann did find some participants who felt they had learned something new. Without exception, however, these were relative newcomers to the Agriculture Department who had not yet learned of the value of budgetary materials for learning about their own agency. Much of what was learned, it became apparent, was not directly related to what they needed, or thought they needed, to do their job. Nonetheless, exposure to the budgetary and programmatic rationale of activities for which they were responsible proved reassuring.

This same pattern appeared in Georgia. Minmier found consistent differences in attitude toward ZBB between budget analysts with experience in both the incremental and zero-base budgeting systems and budget analysts who had worked with only the new zero-base procedures. In general, the newer, less-experienced analysts felt more comfortable with ZBB, while the older analysts had more negative attitudes toward it. The new analysts may simply have been using ZBB as "on the job" training which the more experienced analysts did not need.[44]

There were also differences in attitude toward ZBB between the departmental budget analysts and the central budget office (OPB) analysts. For example, the staff analysts tended more to think that the quality of management information had improved under ZBB and they were more inclined to continue the ZBB system in its current fashion.[45] These response differences could be taken to indicate that ZBB was working: the staff analysts in the OPB were finding ZBB useful in controlling the departments and the departments were resisting this control. But Minmier's study contains a clue that something else may have been happening, for one respondent wrote on his questionnaire:

> The entire Budget Bureau staff which originally implemented zero-base has left the Budget Bureau and the present staff has little experience with zero-base [budgeting] . . .[46]

Minmier nowhere comments on such a turnover in the OPB. Either this respondent was in error, or else Minmier's questionnaire was being answered by OPB staff members who were themselves quite new to the ZBB process and who also may have been using ZBB as part of their "on the job" training.

On the federal level, there were also numerous claims made that going through the ZBB process was a great educational experience. President Carter referred to this in his budget message in 1978: "As a result of the first year's effort [with ZBB], we have gained a better understanding of federal programs and have made better, more even-handed judgments." And for those officials new to their agencies— which means virtually all top officials in the year-old Carter Administration—this was undoubtedly the case.[47] But it would not be unfair to suggest that essentially *everything* they were doing in their first year was giving them quite an education, as is usual in new administrations.[48] It is also not unreasonable to suggest that they would have learned the same things under the old budgetary procedures, which to them would also have been "new."

In their article on the Agriculture Department, Wildavsky and Hammann reported that there were employees who declared they had learned nothing new, but still approved of ZBB anyway. To them the benefits of ZBB were that *others* learned from the effort: department people felt sure that the people down in the agencies had benefitted, while agency people felt sure that the people up at the departmental level had benefitted.

Minmier's account does provide hints that some budgeters in Georgia held such attitudes. One budget analyst, for example, wrote: "In my opinion, zero-base budgeting does serve a very useful cause since it makes someone in the agency review what is going on in the various sections."[49] Somewhat better support for this "it's good for someone else" effect comes from the NASA and Consumer Product Safety Commission appropriations hearings in early 1977. Commenting on the reactions of Appropriations Subcommittee Chairman Boland (D-Mass) and Congressman Max Baucus (D-Mont), who instigated the ZBB experiment with the two agencies, Arlen J. Large of *The Wall Street Journal* wrote:

> So the experiment has shown to the satisfaction of Reps. Boland and Baucus that zero-base budgeting's greatest potential impact will occur in the bureaucracy "downtown" before the budget ever reaches Capitol Hill.[50]

Since in the hearings the responses of both NASA and CPSC officials was pretty much that 'ZBB is a fine management tool, but it didn't really change much in our budget,' it is likely that these officials felt the exercise to be of greater utility in informing Congress of the details of their activities than in changing the activities themselves.

ZBB As a Political Tool

The final unintended role for ZBB that Wildavsky and Hammann found in the Agriculture Department was its use as a political tool. The use of managerial techniques as political tools is an understudied phenomenon. Let us, for the moment, ignore all pretensions of rationality by ZBB, PPBS, MBO, and performance budgeting and simply look upon them as siblings in a family of techniques that newly-appointed top executives use to gain control of their organizations.

The key problem for these people is how can they exercise some measure of control over their bureaucracy? One way is to have their own personal staff take on the bulk of the work involved in formulating and implementing new programs. This was the technique used by Robert Kennedy as Attorney General from 1961 through 1963 in getting the Justice Department—including most importantly the Federal Bureau of Investigation—to do something about organized crime and civil rights violations in the South, neither of which J. Edgar Hoover wanted the FBI to have anything to do with.[51] But top staffers can quickly become bogged down in the effort of doing what the bureaucracy, with its vast resources of expertise, time, and manpower, could do far more easily if it so desired.

It is here that managerial "techniques" may often be used by new executives to bolster their effectiveness. If the techniques appear to embody rationality, as most people think of it, so much the better.[52] If the technique also involves a wholesale disruption of the normal, routine way of doing business, the credence given to "rational" procedures plus the scramble to master the intricate details of the new techniques may hold the bureaucracy at bay while the newcomers learn something about their job. This would be especially true if they themselves are already masters of the technique, as was the case with a number of Robert McNamara's "whiz kids" in the Systems Analysis Office in the Pentagon. From this perspective, it matters not what the particular technique is, as long as it appears rational, as long as it is comprehensive enough, and as long as it is complex enough to keep the bureaucrats off balance for a while.[53]

The manifest purpose of the management techniques—more "rational" decisions, greater efficiency in government, and so forth—will almost inevitably not be achieved. The bureaucrats, finding the techniques less rational and less useful than expected, will master and manipulate them so that decisions will be made in ways little different from before.[54] But meanwhile the new leadership has accomplished two things: it has mastered the politics of the subject matter; and it has learned some of the intricacies of the substantive problems which the bureaucracy handles.[55]

Such uses of managerial techniques are internally-oriented. The techniques can also be used by the agency to deal with external threats. This was precisely the role that the well-known management technique called PERT—Program Evaluation and Review Technique—played in the development of the Polaris missile submarine system in the 1950s and 1960s.[56] The Navy's Special Projects Office which managed the project, and which did a good job for reasons entirely unrelated to PERT, used the technique's complex, rationalistic, and impressive appearance largely to fend off attempts by others to interfere with the project's development. "Those who use such up-to-date techniques must know what they're doing" was the impression the Special Projects Office sought to convey, and the SPO's managerial autonomy was in fact thereby maintained.

Zero-base budgeting can be used to similar effect. Officials in the Department of Agriculture found ZBB to be of use in their relations with the Bureau of the Budget and Congress. An agency which has subjected its own budget to a zero-base review, Wildavsky and Hammann were told, can "truthfully" state to the Bureau and Appropriations Committees that the budget had been examined "from the ground up" and that there is nothing to cut. Agencies discovered such benefits even in their relationships with their superiors in the Department. An old-timer confided to Wildavsky and Hammann that:

> When new administrators come in, they see things they didn't know the Department of Agriculture was doing. They figure this is just the top of the iceberg and get worried. If you take the whole iceberg out of the water and drop it on their desks, and they're too overwhelmed to look at it, they don't have an excuse to nag you anymore. This is the major benefit from the agency point of view: to the extent that their superiors looked at the stuff they were reassured; to the extent they didn't, they no longer have an excuse to nag them [the agencies]."[57]

We would be remiss if we failed to mention zero-base budgeting's use in electoral politics. A candidate brandishing a managerial technique whose name has "tremendous intrinsic appeal" (as Cheek refers to ZBB) can use it to help him get elected.[58] Jimmy Carter is of course the prime example of this. A pledge to "zero-base" the budget is one of a large family of "efficiency in government" pledges which are standard campaign fare. Such pledges are something we expect from candidates. From this perspective, ZBB is our modern-day link to an old political tradition.

People Like Zero-Base Budgeting Mostly Because They Aren't Really Doing It

In the previous pages, we have been trying to come to an understanding of why some participants in the budgetary process retain positive feelings about zero-base budgeting even though most claims made for it remain unfulfilled. Although we have advanced a number of reasons for the persistence of such attitudes, underlying them all is one important fact: these people have positive attitudes toward ZBB *because they aren't doing ZBB*. Considerable evidence shows that ZBB's procedures were not functioning as they should. Instead, what was happening was that people were turning zero-base budgeting into incremental budgeting.[59]

Minmier's study offers some direct evidence that incremental budgeting was being practiced in Georgia. One departmental budget analyst commented that, "In our agency we are actually utilizing incremental budgeting. Our analyst only looks at the packages that come at and just above the 100% level. He only looks at the increments above 100%." Another analyst, after explaining that ZBB requires one to start anew every year, exclaimed: ". . . one cannot start anew with existing operations going on."[60]

One problem was that the size and complexity of agencies prevented thorough reviews of the requested amounts, especially for the essential programs. This led an analyst to argue: ". . . much of the present budgeting is approving continuation of existing expense and very little effort is made toward justifying the existence of the function." Another analyst agreed with this view in confessing that "The mass of paperwork is so complicated and detailed that, as a practical matter, one has to prepare the budget on the basis of the former incremental system for the activity and then break it down into decision packages." An analyst who considered ZBB to have been a worthwhile experiment and advocated its continuance with some modifications, nonetheless concluded that, ". . . we have and are still operating on an incremental budgeting system." As mentioned earlier, most of the original budgeting staff which had instituted ZBB in Georgia was reported to have left the administration; the analyst who made this statement said the newcomers "appear to be evaluating on the basis of incremental [budgeting]."[61]

Due to the large volume of decision packages, even Governor Carter may have succumbed to incremental practices. In Peter Pyhrr's own words, the Governor in 1971

> concentrated on the summary analyses and reviews provided by his financial staff in the Budget Bureau. He had a review with each agency, and concentrated his time on reviewing policy questions, major increases and decreases in existing programs, new programs and capital expenditures, and a few specific packages and rankings where there appeared to be problems.[62]

This doesn't sound much like zero-base budgeting, and in fact, Aaron Wildavsky has pointed out the close similarity between Carter's practices and those of a predecessor, Governor Carl Sanders, from 1962 to 1966. Wildavsky quotes from a study of budgeting in Georgia under Governor Sanders:

> The Budget Bureau prepares a "Summary of Agency Requests for Increase in State Funds" which outlines the major increases requested by each department. . . . It serves as the major guide to consideration of the budget by the Governor. . . . The Governor favored supporting established programs at a level that would allow progress. New programs of less than immediate need were quickly eliminated . . .[63]

Pyhrr's description was of Governor Carter in 1971. Three years later, a departmental budget analyst complained to Minmier that an OPB analyst, "with instructions from his supervisor, did considerable trimming of our [FY-1975] estimated requirements on the premise that the Governor now wants to submit a budget for requirements on a 'continuation of FY-1974' basis."[64] Governor Carter was behaving in a seemingly incremental fashion in 1971; by 1974, if this analyst is to be believed, the Governor was asking the rest of the government to behave that way too.

We cannot tell how prevalent such views and practices were among Georgia's budget analysts, but such comments do point in a clear direction. If this apparent pattern of incremental decision-making was, in fact, widespread in Georgia, then we can conclude that the entire state government—*from top to bottom*—was engaging in incremental budgeting, despite the zero-base name and the zero-base procedures.

Georgia was not unique: Hogan's discussion of ZBB's first year in Texas leads us to suspect that what was happening in Georgia was also happening in Texas. We have already cited Hogan's comments that agencies were using "minimums" and "alternatives" mostly to justify current activities, as well as his comment that there was widespread agreement on the desiribility of formulating current-level-of-effort decision packages. In addition, Hogan noticed a tendency on the part of Texas budget examiners to orient their decisions around the "base," remarking that "examiners found it necessary to recommend either increases or decreases around the basic level of funding where their program and/or activity analysis was centered."[65]

We suspect a more detailed look than Hogan took would show an even more extensive pattern of orientation toward current activities and the current level of funding. LaFaver's article on ZBB in New Mexico likewise noted a similar trend in the state's ZBB effort toward incremental procedures. The major modification for the FY 1974 budget "was the abandonment of the level of effort below the present base. Thus, a rigidly defined base was the first level of effort and expansion items only were ranked in priority order."[66]

The 1976-1977 experiments with ZBB in the EPA, NASA, and the Consumer Product Safety Commission offer no evidence that anything other than incremental budgeting occurred.[67] The EPA, for example, tried to rank all its decision packages from the three major areas in the Energy/Environment Program but was unable to do so. The senior staff involved did, however, attempt to rank a limited subset of packages, those within a range of $10 million above and below the $96 million requested in President Ford's FY 1978 budget. This proved to be "considerably easier" for two reasons. First, "the relationships among the outputs of the several funding increments could be more easily understood." Second, "the impact of adding or deleting the outputs associated with those increments could be compared with the impact of higher priority parts of the program." The EPA Report then went on to explain that "[t]his comparison at the margin is especially important in evaluating budget allocations in a complex inter-related program."[68] In other words, the EPA resorted to incremental budgeting in order to make ZBB work.

The drawing up of the FY 1979 federal budget, the first that required the use of ZBB by all departments, also provides abundant evidence for the persistence of traditional, incremental budgeting. A *New York Times* reporter referred to one Washington-experienced budget official who felt that ZBB did make some "inroads" and did have "some good effects," but who also felt that "incrementalism—how much do we spend above last year's levels—is still the way we do things."[69] The *National Journal* interviewed several budget chiefs; one Treasury budgeter said that, regardless of the talk about going back to zero, "we're really nibbling at the margins." Another budget chief, who asked not to be identified, declared "Zero, shmero . . . It's incremental budgeting."[70]

The Defense Department, for example, did not attempt to justify most bases, ships, and planes. "We didn't get into forces structure and base structure," said one DOD financial official. That might have involved, he explained to the *Times'* reporter, asking the Air Force if it could get along with 24 wings instead of 26 or asking the Army whether Fort Dix in New Jersey or Fort Ord in California was more important to keep open. Instead, he said, "We identified things at the margin," referring to programs that could relatively easily be expanded or contracted, such as production schedules and the rate inventories should be filled. (Construction of big and bulky items such as aircraft carriers was suggested as not being included in these marginal calculations.)[71] ZBB had a similar kind of usefulness at the Commerce Department, where it was said to have helped the Department decide how many mothballed merchant ships to repaint in the upcoming year.

In the Department of Health, Education, and Welfare, a spending band was identified which included items representing spending from ninety percent to 105 percent of current services levels. Those items below the band (items from zero to ninety percent of current services) were all included in the highest priority category. Those above the band were included in the lowest. With this kind of system, notes on HEW budgeter, ZBB focused attention on marginal changes. Amusingly enough, he even argues that "ZBB focused more attention upon marginal changes, up and down, than in the past."[72]

Finally, in summarizing agency responses to the OMB's survey on the utility of ZBB in preparing the 1979 budgets, Draper and Pitsvada note that

> . . . some mention should be made of the fact that the responses reenforce the idea that ZBB is as much incremental budgeting as anything else. . . . For in the final analysis, most important decisions on resource allocation questions *are* decisions made at the margin. As such, proponents and practitioners of ZBB should seek to trade on its ability to inject a form of marginal utility analysis into budget preparation.[73]

Wherever we look, within the severe limits of the secondary-source data, it appears that people are not *doing* zero-base budgeting even though they may be *calling* it that. So if some people like ZBB but what they are doing is incrementalism, then it may be that the reason they like ZBB is *because* they are doing incrementalism.

Peter Pyhrr on Incremental Zero-Base Budgeting

If incrementalism is pervasive in the organizations using ZBB, are ZBB proponents such as Pyhrr and Cheek aware of it? After all, as management consultants they have considerable experience with the organizations trying to use ZBB. Problems with ZBB did appear even in Pyhrr's earliest application of ZBB in Texas Instruments, and these problems gave rise to several adaptations, deletions, and additions to the ZBB format. While Pyhrr was sensitive to such problems, he does not seem to recognize that his adaptations and modifications, when taken together, constitute a major retreat from the "examine everything" spirit of zero-base review.[74]

How can we decide what next year's level of funding should be? What activities should we support? Pyhrr suggests that *"[a] logical starting point for determining next year's needs is the current year's operations."*[75] It also helps if the central budget office issues general guidelines "as to realistic expenditure levels for the coming budget year." Such guidelines provide managers with a "uniform basis for viewing the coming year . . ."[76] With these various assumptions, managers can identify their " 'business as usual' levels of effort." These steps provide managers with "a necessary orientation and background analysis" before decision packages are even prepared.[77]

How should managers handle the problem of ranking large numbers of packages? Pyhrr suggests that managers should limit "the number of consolidation levels to which the packages will be merged."[78] But limiting the number of consolidated packages leaves a considerable portion of the budget unranked. The decisions of middle and upper-level managers on where to allocate money will thus have to be made as they were before ZBB was adopted.

How should managers cope with the problem of examining large numbers of decision packages? If next year's expenditures are going to be similar to this year's, management should focus its attention on the packages whose proposed expenditures lie "between 80% and some level in excess of 100%."[79] When the anticipated spending level for next year exceeds the current year's level by a considerable amount, Pyhrr advises that ". . . we do not want to spend too much time concentrating on the absolute priority of packages from the 80 to 100% levels."[80] Instead, it is the priority of packages around the expected funding level that is important: management should concentrate its review "on lower priority or discretionary packages around which the funding levels or cutoff will be determined."[81] In other words, budgeters are supposed to concentrate their attention on changes from current operations, which is how budgeting is usually done anyway.

A question arises as to whether Pyhrr's recommendations—base this year's needs on last year's, premise decisions on general funding guidelines, limit the number of consolidated rankings, concentrate on discretionary and low priority packages—represent a form of modified zero-base review or whether they reduce ZBB to good old run-of-the-mill incrementalism. Allen Schick noted in a 1977 article that zero-base budgeting "in practice . . . is more a form of marginal analysis than a requirement that the budget be built up from scratch each year."[82] But as far as we can tell, Schick's discussion of ZBB is not based on the "modified version" we have just described but on the original "examine and justify everything" procedures. We leave it up to the reader to decide as to how Schick would characterize ZBB when all of Pyhrr's qualifications are taken into account.

Is Incremental Budgeting Mindless?

If incrementalism is pervasive in organizations using zero-base budgeting, and ZBB proponents themselves unknowingly adopt incremental practices, why does the idea of incrementalism come under such continual attack?

The most common criticism of traditional, incremental budgeting is that it is essentially mindless. In this view, only desires for annual increases in personnel and supplies are taken into account, and there is no analysis of benefits gained by these expenditures. Logan Cheek presents a particularly overdrawn version of traditional budgeting:[83]

- All ongoing expenditures are taken as essential. The base itself is not examined.
- Future expenditures are calculated only by taking the base and adding to it adjustments for inflation and hoped-for increases in old and new programs.
- Attention is focused only on increments to the base.
- Once a program is started, it is never terminated.
- Programs are not compared to see if resources should be shifted from the less to the more productive.
- Budget submissions are padded to account for expected cuts.
- When budgets need cutting, no one knows how to avoid cutting "muscle" instead of "fat," so arbitrary, across-the-board cuts are made.
- It is assumed that all ongoing projects are being efficiently managed.
- Even when formal long-range planning is done, it is not integrated into budgeting.

Is this a realistic picture of traditional, line-item budgeting? To be sure, some elements are a reasonable sketch. Attention *is* focused (though not solely) on increments to the base;[84] "padding" *does* go on. There may be instances in which increments have been added to programs which themselves are not worth funding. But to say that programs are seldom examined and evaluated is incorrect. More thought, study, analysis, comparison, and justification go into budgetary calculation than Cheek's dismal picture allows for. That this examination and evaluation is often routine and informal simply means that closer inspection is needed to reveal their occurrence.[85]

The ZBB literature itself has clues that traditional budgeting is not devoid of evaluation. In some states, it was the very desire to evaluate programs which caused them to try the zero-base budgeting method. As the experience in New Mexico illustrates, several programs not coming under ZBB requirements were also cut and revamped. In other words, the incentive and capability to analyze the budgetary base existed independently of, and prior to, the adoption of zero-base budgeting procedures. One Georgia budget official felt there were similar opportunities for change in Governor Carter's Georgia budget even without ZBB; he insisted that "[t]here was, prior to this [zero-base] budget process and still are, ways in which to redirect program efforts and expenditures of funds."[86]

Traditional budget outcomes also vary much more than ZBB proponents seem to think. Budgets are not just simple extrapolations from the past to the future. In testimony to the House Budget Committee in 1976, Allen Schick argued that while "many people insist that if something is placed in the budget, it never leaves the budget . . . ," in fact "there has been a turnover in programs." "It is," he said, ". . . a simplification to insist that nothing gets removed from the base if it already is in the budget" and he observed that:

> If one were to look at the budget of the United States of a decade ago, and lay it side by side with the budget for fiscal 1977, we would find a considerable number of programs which now are funded at a lower level than they were a decade ago, or at a lower level in terms of constant dollars, and we would also find a number of programs which were in the budget 10 years ago and no longer are there."

Not only do programs come and go. They also change, Schick continued:

> We also will tend to find, if we were to place these programs under the microscope, so that we could look at them in more minute pieces, that even though the total program level does not appear to change, there are within Federal agencies constant redirections of effort.[87]

As Schick suggests, spending patterns *within* agencies may vary much more than total agency budgets. Natchez and Bupp, for example, found that expenditures on specific programs and policies in one federal agency showed a good deal of variation.[88] Programs prospered or declined depending on the abilities of individual program directors to build political support for their programs and to protect them from competing claims on their resources. Similarly, in Gist's study of line-item expenditures in several agency budgets, it was discovered that not all parts of the budget change to the same degree nor move in the same direction; budgeters were making choices—that is, setting priorities—even without formal ranking procedures.[89]

These changes in priorities reflect, in good measure, changes in the political forces around agencies and programs. In his study of the appropriations process in Congress, Richard Fenno found that two key political variables—*congressional* support for an agency and *public* support for the agency—could account for different patterns of growth and susceptibility to budget cuts among federal agencies. Budget requests by agencies popular with the public rose rapidly, but unless they were also popular with Congress, their requests were likely to be cut back considerably. Budget requests by agencies popular with Congress but with no visible public constituency were not likely to grow rapidly,

but their requests were seldom cut by the House Appropriations Committee.[90] Using more sophisticated statistical techniques, Davis,
Dempster, and Wildavsky found broad-gauge changes in expenditure
patterns which could be attributed to political factors such as which
party controlled Congress and the presidency, to changes in the political environment of an agency, to the passage of new laws and changes
in old ones, to agency reorganization, and to a variety of economic
factors.[91]

Although the changes in the rates of growth found in these programs
nonetheless seem undramatic, we might point out that even the most
modest rates of growth in a program can quickly add up to big changes.
A program growing at a steady seven percent per year (compounded
annually) *doubles* its size in about ten and one-half years.[92] If this
steady growth is occurring in a worthwhile program, a doubling in size
in ten years is not an insignificant shift of resources if less worthwhile
programs are not growing as fast. If we take two equal-sized programs,
with one growing at seven percent a year and the other at four percent,
at the end of five years the four percent program is only about eighty-
seven percent the size of the other. And if the growth of the seven
percent program is taking place *at the direct expense of the other program*, at the end of five years the shrinking program is only about
forty-three percent the size of the other one. Little yearly shifts in
allocations can thus result in big changes in priorities. This lesson is
mundane, but too often overlooked.

Understanding the importance of political support for budgetary
changes also provides us with an explanation for why some agencies'
budgets do seem quite stable. Instead of positing a mindless and au-
tomatic incrementalism which produces unchanging budgets, it may be
more accurate to say that there is an *equilibrium* of contending forces
in the political competition for funds. That is, in each year's budget the
appearance of stability may be the product of a stable balance of power
among the major participants—the agencies, the OMB, the President,
and the Congress. As this underlying balance changes, the budget
changes accordingly. Thus we can explain changes in the proportion
of the federal budget going to military and social welfare activities in
the past fifteen years as reflecting broad changes in the political power
and preferences of presidents, congressmen, and the public. When
these underlying forces change, the budget changes; when the relative
strengths of the forces are stable, the budget is stable. Stability thus
may not reflect *mindlessness* on the part of the agencies so much as
the political *constraints* on them: they want more, but they can't get
it.[93]

The Costs of Trying ZBB: Looking Rational Versus Being Rational

Traditional, incremental budgeting has a few more virtues than ZBB proponents seem to recognize, and ZBB has a few more faults than its proponents care to admit. In fact, attempting to do zero-base budgeting is a *costly* enterprise in a variety of ways.

Wildavsky and Hammann calculated that the Department of Agriculture's effort in the early 1960s cost some 180,000 man-hours of work and *perhaps* led to some $200,000 in budget changes, a return, they noted, of slightly over a dollar per hour for their work.[94] NASA's Administrator estimated that his agency's FY 1978 ZBB effort, which covered only the Research and Program Development (R.&P.D.) part of its budget, cost "on the order of $200,000."[95] The R.&P.D. account was only some twenty-one percent of NASA's entire budget request for FY 1978.

Perhaps if ZBB were the only budget system in operation, that is, if it completely supplanted the current system, costs might be no larger than under the current system. But if the frank comments of some of Georgia's departmental budget analysts are to be believed, Georgia had a dual budgeting system despite the fact that ZBB was the only *official* system. To the extent that there is such an informal system, time and money are being spent to operate it, in addition to the work involved in converting its output into the ZBB format.

Some observers of the FY 1979 budget process contend that ZBB has not created a dual budgeting system in the federal government.[96] Participants in the process have likewise claimed that ZBB has become *the* budgetary procedure, not just an add-on to how things are really done. But extensive elements of the previous system have remained part of the process. As one budget analyst with the Department of Housing and Urban Development described HUD's budget submission, "The ZBB part of the submission was, after all, an add-on to the financial tables, supporting documentation, and traditional justifications that continues to be required" by the OMB.[97] When submissions did not adequately highlight important budget issues, the OMB resorted to its traditional "issue papers" or "forced" the issue to fit into the required ZBB format.[98] Consequently, though ZBB may have become more central to the decision process than PPBS did in the 1960s, much of what went on before still goes on, and the overall financial costs of running the budgeting process have undoubtedly increased.

The ZBB operation also produced huge amounts of paperwork for many, though not all, agencies.[99] Most budget officers who had worked with PPBS, a system known for its deluge of paper, felt that ZBB's "paper load" was about twice as much as under PPBS.[100] *The Wall Street Journal* wrote that there was, government-wide, a "huge increase in paperwork, estimated at 50%."[101] The Environmental Protection Agency was reported by *The New York Times* as feeling "suffocated by paper,"[102] and it is estimated, for example, that the amount of paperwork in the Department of Housing and Urban Development was double that of the 1978 budget process.[103]

Besides the financial costs, there are a number of *political* costs. Forcing people to agree on objectives can lead to overt conflict where there was none previously. Similarly, forcing administrators to rank activities and programs in order of priority can cause conflict over priorities where there was little previously. Reliance on quantitative performance measures can result in goal displacement (or, shall we say, *more* goal displacement than already occurs in government agencies). And if the "income effect" is not dealt with adequately, agencies may be required to resubmit their budgetary proposals a number of times. If resubmission requires further negotiation and the disruption of just-concluded agreements, budgetary conflict may extend further into the fiscal year.

Finally, there are *opportunity* costs. In HUD, ZBB used three or four times the amount of staff and top management hours that are normally used. Yet top management complained that they should have had more time to adequately go through the ZBB steps.[104] In the Consumer Product Safety Commission the ZBB process "consumed a sizable portion of limited resources," according to the comptroller, and "dominated the time and efforts of the commission's managerial staff and their subordinates for almost three months."[105] One Environmental Protection Agency official who liked ZBB nevertheless complained that "The demands on my staff were unreal."[106] Another EPA staff member warned of the dangers of getting too absorbed in budgeting at the cost of actually protecting the environment. "We spent so much time on the budget," he said, "that a lot of other things slipped."[107] As Draper and Pitsvada warn, ". . . the opportunity costs of greater management participation were high in some cases."[108]

In Congress' own initial encounter with ZBB, some of these same opportunity costs were incurred. The NASA-House Appropriations Subcommittee ZBB effort is a case in point. In response to a number of serious problems in the Space Shuttle program—engineering difficulties, delays in European construction of the manned space laboratory, Space Shuttle fleet size questions, increasing payload costs, and possible deleterious effects of Space Shuttle booster rockets on the upper atmosphere—the House Appropriations Committee assigned a team of staff members to thoroughly analyze these problems. The resulting report (unrelated to the ZBB experiment) was some seventy-eight pages long. The actual hearings based on the staff report resulted in only fifteen pages of testimony, and the committee's questioning was less than thorough. The inconclusive ZBB hearing, however, consumed fifty-one pages of testimony, though the ZBB effort could not be regarded as being of comparable importance to the substantive questions raised by the staff about the Space Shuttle program.

It may be that for those congressmen and executive branch managers who are concerned mainly with *looking* rational, adopting ZBB fits the bill. For those interested in *being* rational, more mundane techniques are called for: master a subject matter and its problems through diligent investigation; try to ameliorate specific problems through discussions, hearings, passage of legislation or whatever; and follow up on the implementation of the reforms to make sure things are done as intended. These are the constituents of rationality in government, unglamorous though they may be.

Are we being unfair to the proponents of zero-base budgeting? After all, they do caution that there are certain preconditions for ZBB to actually work. Governor Carter, for example, once stated that:

> Zero-base budgeting has proved its value for those organizations endowed with a will to manage, to engage in a productive dialogue founded on mutual trust during tough planning and budgeting decisions, and to find new and better ways to serve their constituents or customers. But like most new management tools, success requires balancing the approach with classic, common sense human-relations and creative problem-solving techniques.[109]

The irony of such qualifications is that if all these preconditions held true, there would be no need whatsoever for zero-base budgeting. For if, as Governor Carter specified, some organization has all these attributes, what could ZBB possibly do for it? If *any* organization is going to succeed at the tasks it sets for itself, *this* organization is going to succeed, ZBB or no ZBB!

These qualifications echo those made by earlier proponents of PPBS and MBO. Wildavsky was driven to observe that ". . . many defenses of PPBS . . . end up alleging, in effect, that the world is not good enough for it. The paradox is that the world PPBS is supposed to change must first undergo that change before it can accommodate PPBS."[110] The same appeared true of an attempt at using MBO in HEW. Administrators were asked what improvements they would make beyond MBO, and they mentioned "management accountability and responsibility . . . better teamwork . . . co-ordination . . . a need for clear mission goals and priorities . . . and the development of management information systems."[111] Of course, as Wildavsky pointed out, these improvements were "exactly what MBO was supposed to accomplish in the first place."[112]

We might end this chapter by reminding the reader that at this writing ZBB has had only one full year in the federal government; foulups, mishaps, and other difficulties, such as we have described here, were to be expected and should be discounted accordingly. But the question remains as to *when* ZBB *will* have an impact. In Georgia what little effect it did have occurred in its first year, according to Minmier's analysis. One federal budget expert who has, according to *The New York Times*, watched presidents come and go for a long time, reflected on when the new budgeting technique might be most useful: "You should get the big payoff in the first two years. By the third year, it probably will be reduced to a routine . . . You will have gotten most of what a new process can give you."[113] If this person was right, ZBB had only one year left to prove its mettle.

This is not to say that President Carter and his administration are having no impact on the federal budget; on the contrary, they began to have an impact on the budget soon after taking office, and are continuing to do so. We have already referred to budgetary changes in the EPA, for example, and we could mention many more, such as the B-1 bomber decision, the energy program, and the elimination of a number of water development projects. And as for the FY 1979 budget's being a lean one, *The Wall Street Journal* wrote that it is not ". . . because of zero-base budgeting, but because Jimmy Carter has insisted upon stringent spending ceilings."[114]

So in seeking the causes of budgetary changes in the Carter Administration, look not at the budgetary techniques being used, but at the President, the men and women he has appointed, the political party to which they belong, and the constituencies they and their bureaucracies all have. It is there that the sources of budgetary change and "reform" will be found.

Notes

1. Pyhrr, *Zero-Base Budgeting*, pp. 32-34.
2. Minmier, *An Evaluation of the Zero-Base Budgeting System in Governmental Institutions*, p. 156.
3. Minmier, pp. 154-55.
4. Minmier, p. 155.

5. Minmier, pp. 156-157. Apparently, however, this "need" for reorganization was perceived by Carter before he had ever heard of ZBB, since he
   had run for governor in 1970 on a platform promising reorganization of
   state government. See page 128 of *Why Not The Best?* Peter Pyhrr's first
   article on ZBB, which alerted the new Governor to the approach, was
   not published until the November-December 1970 issue of *The Harvard
   Business Review*. Recent interviews in Georgia substantiate our skepticism. One agency budget officer who served on the reorganization team
   in 1971 has been quoted as saying, "We had already identified duplication
   and proliferation of agencies by the time the first ZBB packages were
   prepared in the summer of 1971—but the packages did reaffirm what had
   been identified by separate investigation." From Thomas P. Lauth, "Zero-
   Base Budgeting In Georgia State Government: Myth and Reality," *Public
   Administration Review* 38 (September/October 1978), p. 426.
6. Minmier, p. 157. Minmier does conclude that ZBB made an "indirect"
   contribution to reallocations, the majority of which occurred during the
   first year of its implementation in connection with the reorganization. We
   suspect that Minmier is being overly charitable in his evaluation of ZBB's
   contribution. At any rate, he presents no evidence for any "indirect"
   ZBB contribution to reallocation other than that Governor Carter said
   ZBB had made a contribution. That resources *were* evidently reallocated
   probably stemmed from the fact that Jimmy Carter had different concerns
   from his predecessor, Lester Maddox.
7. See Lauth, "Zero-Base Budgeting in Georgia State Government,"
   pp. 423-425.
8. This first year of ZBB did not utilize the full paraphernalia of Pyhrr's
   version of ZBB. As such, the first year's effort was more akin to that of
   the U.S. Department of Agriculture in 1961-1963, described by Aaron
   Wildavsky and Arthur Hammann in "Comprehensive Versus Incremental
   Budgeting in the Department of Agriculture," *Administrative Science
   Quarterly* 10 (December 1965). The more elaborate version was adopted
   in New Mexico in later years.
9. LaFaver, "Zero Base Budgeting in New Mexico," *State Government* 47
   (Spring 1974), p. 108.
10. Michael J. Scheiring, "Zero-Based Budgeting in New Jersey," pp. 374
    and 378 of *Compendium*. Scheiring does comment that while "Few bud-
    get decisions could clearly be attributed to the zero-base" approach, an
    interview with Budget Bureau official indicated that ZBB was "a definite
    factor in influencing many of the budget decisions that were made." See
    page 378 in *Compendium*. Unfortunately, Scheiring offered no further
    information to back up this statement, and it is again difficult to know
    what to think.
11. David W. Singleton, Bruce A. Smith, and James R. Cleaveland, "Zero-
    Based Budgeting in Wilmington, Delaware," *The Bureaucrat* 6 (Spring
    1977): 67-87.
12. Ibid, p. 78.
13. Draper and Pitsvada, *A First Year Assessment*, p. 32.
14. "ZBB in the Federal Government," p. 8.
15. Allen Schick, "The Road From ZBB," *Public Administration Review* 38
    (March/April 1978), pp. 177, 178.

16. Edward Cowan, "Zero-Base Budgeting—It Made A Difference," *The New York Times*, January 22, 1978, Section 3, p. 14.
17. Lefford B. Fauntleroy, Jr., "Reflections on ZBB: A Congressional Test and the Executive Mandate," *The Bureaucrat* 7 (April 1978), p. 14.
18. See William J. Eaton, "Zero-Base Budgeting—Some Say It's Nothing," *San Francisco Sunday Examiner-Chronicle*, January 15, 1978, Section C, p. 13.
19. Gina Bari Kolata, "National Bureau of Standards: A Fall From Grace," *Science* 197 (2 September 1977).
20. R. Jeffrey Smith, "Carter Budget Tilts 'Back to Basics' For Research," *Science* 199 (3 February 1978), p. 509.
21. This account by Joel Havemann is the only adequate account of ZBB in action on the FY 1979 federal budget so far. See "The Tale of How One Agency Used ZBB—And Lived to Tell About It," *National Journal* 10 (18 February 1978), p. 265.
22. Ibid, p. 265.
23. See also Farney, "Birth Pains," p. 1.
24. Havemann, "The Tale," p. 267.
25. Eaton, "Zero-base Budgeting," p. 13.
26. Havemann, "The Tale," p. 266-267.
27. Smith, "Carter Budget," p. 509.
28. Havemann, "The Tale," pp. 265, 269.
29. See, for example, Luther J. Carter, "Toxic Substances: Five Year Struggle For Landmark Bill May Soon Be Over," *Science* 194 (1 October 1976).
30. Havemann, "The Tale," p. 267.
31. One can argue, in fact, that the increase in the EPA's budget is *33%*, if President Ford's original 1978 proposals are used as the basis of comparison, instead of President Carter's revisions of the Ford 1978 budget. President Ford's 1977 EPA budget was $783,705,000. His 1978 recommendation was $848,803,000, and President Carter, just taking office at the time, increased this (through supplemental requests, for example) to some $1,003,603,000. His own 1979 request was for $1,127,600,000. So the 1979 budget is about 33% larger than President Ford's last request, though only about 12% more than the joint Ford-Carter 1978 budget. Probably the figure most expressive of President Carter's great environmental concern is the fact that by the end of 1979, he will have increased the EPA budget by almost 44% in only two years.
32. Cowan, "Zero-Base Budgeting," p. 14.
33. Farney, "Birth Pains," p. 22.
34. Peter Pyhrr has recently stated that, "If we can't realistically expect major funding reallocations among major agencies, and if we can't expect a tax decrease, then why do zero-base budgeting?" His answer is that any major reallocations that do occur will take place *within* major agencies. (See his "The Zero-Base Approach to Government Budgeting," p. 8.) But the evidence gives no support for even this notion. For example, William A. Eckert, analyzing *within-department* budget categories in the Georgia ZBB budget through 1975, concluded that ZBB did not signifi-

cantly alter outcomes here either. See his "Evaluating The Impact of Zero-Base Budgeting," unpublished paper presented at the Annual Meeting of the Midwest Political Science Association, Chicago, Illinois, April 20-22, 1978. Cited by Thomas P. Lauth, "Zero-Base Budgeting in Georgia State Government," p. 425.

35. Minmier, *An Evaluation*, pp. 118-121. The raw numbers were recalculated from Minmier's percentages.
36. Draper and Pitsvada, *A First Year Assessment*, p. 11.
37. This is a different conclusion from that drawn by Minmier who said, "there has been little evidence discovered indicating any reduction in the efficiency of the State's budgeting process as a result of employing the zero-base budgeting system." See page 170. But to Minmier, greater involvement in and of itself is a good thing. It was "discouraging" to him to find that several department heads were reported as not becoming more involved in budgeting. See page 118 for his views.
38. Minmier, p. 167.
39. Ibid.
40. See Wildavsky and Hammann, "Comprehensive Versus Incremental Budgeting in the Department of Agriculture."
41. Ibid, p. 153.
42. Knott's research on the politics of fiscal policy in West Germany uncovered a similar process at work: West German budget officials had a much greater appreciation for Chancellor Schmidt, who is very interested in budgets, than they had had for former Chancellor Willy Brandt, who wasn't.
43. Cheek, *Zero-Base Budgeting Comes of Age*, p. 162, emphasis added.
44. An additional factor may have been that the newcomers to Georgia state government were people who were recruited by the Carter Administration and who, therefore, identified more with Governor Carter than with the agency in which they were placed. These recruits may have closely identified with their boss and his budgeting policies. Veterans in the state agencies, who were there before Carter became governor and who were likely to be there after Carter left, would have felt no such compulsion to think highly of ZBB. Minmier presents no information with which we can evaluate this hypothesis, and it must remain just that. Another reason for appearing to approve of ZBB might simply be reporting bias: respondents might have wanted to appear to investigators as "rational" and "up-to-date" in management practices.
45. See Minmier, Item 11, p. 235 and Item 14, p. 236. In 1978 Lauth reported that Georgia budgeters still feel this way ("Zero-Base Budgeting in Georgia State Government," p. 427), and Blandin and Donahue of the OMB think that ZBB provided "more and better information" about agency programs in the federal government ("ZBB: Not A Panacea," p. 54).
46. See Minmier, Appendix K, p. 258.
47. Ranking of the EPA's 550 decision packages, for example, was done by six assistant administrators, none of whom had been on the job more than a few months, and by a deputy regional administrator. One of the six commented that he and his colleagues were united by "a common level of ignorance." See Havemann, "The Tale," p. 268.

48. The *National Journal*, for example, in speaking of the "huge chunks" of time required by the ZBB process, said that, "This proved useful to the assistant administrators, who were brand new to EPA when the budget season reached peak intensity last summer. Zero-base budgeting provided them with a crash course in the activities of their new organization." In Havemann, "The Tale," p. 267.
49. Minmier, p. 262.
50. "Applying Zero-Base Budgeting," *The Wall Street Journal*, May 24, 1977, p. 20.
51. See Victor Navasky, *Kennedy Justice* (New York: Atheneum, 1970), Chapters 1-3.
52. Unless, of course, the bureaucrats have heard many such claims and seen many such techniques come and go. In this case skepticism may prevail. Scheiring leads us to think that this occurred in ZBB's implementation in New Jersey. The state had had an earlier and not very successful experience with PPBS (see page 372 of Scheiring's account), and Scheiring noted their predictable reaction to ZBB: "Many agency personnel expressed the opinion that ZBB was just a glossy public relations gimmick. They felt that much of the information demands placed upon them would not enter the picture when it came time to make budget decisions, either by the agency internally, by the central budget office, or by the Governor's office in making budget recommendations to the Legislature." See "Zero-Based Budgeting in New Jersey," pp. 377-8 in *Compendium*.
53. For their own part, the old-timers in the Department of Agriculture also found they could use the new procedures to advantage. Some officials discovered that programs which they had desired for several years received added impetus when they could say that the zero-base analysis supported their views. "[H]aving proposed the change they had in mind," Wildavsky and Hammann wrote, "the responsible officials could use the belief that the zero-base approach was more rational to make their colleagues more amenable to the change." See Wildavsky and Hammann, p. 156.
54. Ralph Sanders, who worked on McNamara's staff in the Department of Defense, notes in his *The Politics of Defense Analysis* (New York: Dunellen, 1973), that the number of systems analysts of one sort or another *in military uniform* in the Defense Department rose from virtually zero in 1961 when McNamara became Secretary to some two hundred by 1970. See pp. 51ff. Sanders states that the competitive position of the military services vis-a-vis the Office of the Secretary of Defense improved greatly as they improved their own analytic capabilities. Sanders even defined some "rules" on how to engage in the 'politics of analysis,' given that under McNamara systems analysis was the language in which policy differences would be worked out: (1) Adhere to the Secretary's idea of what constitutes good systems analysis; (2) Use your methodology to ferret out the methodology, assumptions, conclusions, and recommendations of opposing groups; (3) Try to maximize the chances of getting one's analysis to the decisionmaker; and (4) Use analysis for winning over allies. See pp. 271ff.

55. Marz makes a similar point in his article on "magic": "Any new budgeting system, no matter what its rationale or ritual, has a transitory latent function. Until the constituent agencies master the new system, it permits the central budget agency to recapture discretion over a larger fraction of total government expenditure. By changing budgetary rules every five or six years the central budget agency can keep the wolves at bay. Since these new systems must have a manifest as well as a latent function, the magical explanation of more economy, improved efficiency or superior rationality comes into play." See Roger Marz, "Myth, Magic and Administrative Innovations," *Administration and Society* 10 (August 1978), p. 137.
56. See the account by Harvey Sapolsky, *The Polaris System Development* (Cambridge, Mass.: Harvard University Press, 1972).
57. Wildavsky and Hammann, p. 161.
58. The benefits to management consultants who push ZBB on unsuspecting clients are measured not in votes but in dollars. This is a latent function of managerial techniques which should not be neglected. And to be honest, of course, we should mention that academics (Hammond and Knott?) also reap some benefits from agencies which adopt managerial techniques that are bound to fail. They can get books and articles published criticizing such foolishness and thereby win job offers, tenure, and if they are especially lucky, their own modicum of riches! That public services are not improved by the good fortune of management consultants and academics is entirely incidental.
59. Wildavsky and Hammann observed the same process at work in the Department of Agriculture's 1962-1963 experiment: ". . . even those who found some use for the zero-base approach began to assimilate it to the more familiar incremental method. They would use it from time to time to 'take inventory,' as one put it, and then take their bearings for the immediate future from that date." See page 157.
60. Minmier, p. 262.
61. Minmier, pp. 264, 263, 264, 258.
62. Pyhrr, *Zero-Base Budgeting*, p. 97.
63. From Augustus B. Turnbull, III, *Politics in the Budgetary Process: The Case of Georgia* (Athens, Georgia: unpublished Ph.D. dissertation, University of Georgia, 1967), pp. 236, 243. Cited by Wildavsky in *Budgeting* (Boston, Mass.: Little, Brown, 1975), p. 295.
64. Minmier, p. 263.
65. Hogan, p. 293.
66. "Zero-Base Budgeting in New Mexico," p. 110 in original, p. 89 in *Compendium*.
67. With the severe time limits all three agencies were operating under—they had already submitted their budgets to OMB under normal procedures—these experiments cannot be regarded as truly valid ZBB exercises.
68. EPA Report, "An Experiment . . . ," pp. 15-16.
69. Cowan, "Zero-Base Budgeting," p. 1.
70. Joel Havemann, "The Budget—A Tax Cut, Little Else," *National Journal* 10 (28 January 1978), p. 129.
71. Cowan, "Zero-Base Budgeting," p. 14.

72. Thomas W. De Hanas, "Zero-base Budgeting and the Management Review Process in the Department of Health, Education and Welfare," *The Bureaucrat* 7 (April 1978), p. 25.
73. Draper and Pitsvada, *A First Year Assessment*, p. 52. Emphasis in original.
74. It is to Peter Pyhrr's credit that he recognized these problems and adapted his procedures to try to meet them. These problems and adaptations were mentioned in passing in his 1970 article, but only elaborated fully in his 1973 book. Most other ZBB proponents, such as Logan Cheek *(Zero-Base Budgeting Comes of Age)* and Stonich *(Zero-Base Planning and Budgeting)* have not learned from experience the way that Peter Pyhrr did. It is for this reason that Pyhrr's 1973 presentation remains the preferred full-length exposition of ZBB.
75. Pyhrr, "Zero-Base Budgeting," p. 114, emphasis added.
76. Pyhrr, *Zero-Base Budgeting*, p. 14.
77. Ibid, p. 14.
78. Ibid, p. 82.
79. Ibid, p. 86.
80. Ibid, pp. 86-87. He doesn't mention, however, what this lack of attention does to the utility of the rankings if expenditures unexpectedly have to be trimmed. Simply moving the cutoff line, as he prescribes, won't work well because priorities around the new cutoff point weren't carefully examined when the rankings were originally made.
81. Ibid, p. 82.
82. "Zero Base Budgeting and Sunset: Redundancy or Symbiosis?" *The Bureaucrat* 6 (Spring 1977), p. 16.
83. The following items were compiled from Logan Cheek, *Zero-Base Budgeting Comes of Age*, pp. viii-ix, 2-8, 16-17. We assume that Cheek is trying to amuse us with other of his attacks on traditional budgeting. For example, he states that a controller's staff, when putting together the final budget "become[s] increasingly frustrated and irritable, which leads to high turnover and morale problems. Extreme cases degenerate into ulcers and divorces . . ." (p. 7). He repeats his little joke on page 17 where he reiterates that traditional budgeting is "known to lead to high turnover and morale problems, not to mention divorces and ulcers." Cheek's table on pages 16 and 17 comparing traditional with zero-base budgeting is the most humorous presentation in the ZBB literature. But since this tongue-in-cheek approach is not in evidence anywhere else in his book, it does make us wonder whether Cheek is perhaps serious after all.
84. As we saw earlier in this chapter, however, this is also descriptive of zero-base budgeting.
85. The kind of "incrementalism" that goes on is actually more akin to what Amitai Etzioni called "mixed-scanning" in his essay, "Mixed-Scanning: A 'Third' Approach to Decision-Making," *Public Administration Review* 27 (December 1967). For empirical evidence on the matter, see Nienaber and Wildavsky, *The Budgeting and Evaluation of Federal Recreation Programs*, chapters 2 and 3.
86. Minmier, p. 263.
87. See Statement of Allen Schick, Congressional Research Service, "Zero-Base Budget Legislation," Hearings Before the Task Force on Budget Process of the Committee on the Budget, House of Representatives, 94th

Congress, Second Session, June 30; July 27 and 28, 1976, pp. 46-47. Schick's comments are reprinted in the appendix of Cheek, *Zero Base Budgeting Comes of Age*, pp. 258-269.

88. Peter B. Natchez and Irvin C. Bupp, "Policy and Priority in the Budgetary Process," *American Political Science Review* 67 (September 1973): 951-963.
89. John R. Gist, "Mandatory Expenditures and the Defense Sector: The Theory of Budgetary Incrementalism," *Sage Professional Papers in American Politics*, Number 04-020 (Beverly Hills, Ca.: Sage Publications, 1974). We should point out that Eckert's analysis of Georgia's budgets up through 1975 does not reveal this kind of fluctuation. See his "Evaluating the Impact of Zero-Base Budgeting," cited by Lauth, "Zero-Base Budgeting in Georgia State Government," p. 425.
90. See Richard F. Fenno's *The Power of the Purse* (Boston, Mass.: Little, Brown, 1966). See also the table and commentary of Francis Rourke on Fenno's data in *Bureaucracy, Politics and Public Policy*, first edition, (Boston, Mass.: Little, Brown, 1969), pp. 24-27.
91. Otto A. Davis, M.A.H. Dempster and Aaron Wildavsky, "Towards A Predictive Theory of Government Expenditure: U.S. Domestic Appropriations," *British Journal of Political Science* 4 (October 1974). These changes were labeled "shift points" in their article.
92. Critics of incremental budgeting actually make this point quite often, but take it only in the negative sense: "With lots of little increases, bad programs can quickly get out of hand" is their only point.
93. These comments are tailored to the problems of governmental budgeting, but we suspect that the formulation of budgets in business firms can accurately be described in the same political sense. See Cyert and March, *A Behavioral Theory of the Firm* and March's article, "The Business Firm As A Political Coalition," *Journal of Politics* 24 (November 1962): 662-678. Bower's study, *Managing The Resource Allocation Process* cited in chapter 2 (footnote 11), provides additional support for this view.
94. Wildavsky and Hammann, "Comprehensive Budgeting in the Department of Agriculture," pp. 161-162.
95. U.S. House of Representatives, Appropriations Hearings, 1977, NASA, pp. 964-965.
96. See, for example, Allen Schick, "The Road From ZBB," *Public Administration Review* 38 (March/April 1978), pp. 177-178.
97. Bruce Conger, "Zero-base Budgeting at the Department of Housing and Urban Development," *The Bureaucrat* 7 (Spring 1978), p. 46.
98. Blandin and Donahue, "ZBB: Not A Panacea," p. 54.
99. Farney, "Birth Pains," p. 22.
100. Richard E. Miller, "ZBB in the Federal Government," p. 6.
101. Farney, "Birth Pains," p. 22.
102. Cowan, "Zero-Base Budgeting," p. 14.
103. Ralph C. Bledsoe, "What Top Managers Ought To Know About ZBB," *The Bureaucrat* 7 (April 1978), p. 58.
104. Ibid.
105. Lefford B. Fauntleroy, "Reflections on ZBB," pp. 13-14.
106. Cowan, "Zero-Base Budgeting," p. 14.
107. Havemann, "The Tale," p. 268.

108. *A First Year Assessment*, p. 12.
109. Jimmy Carter, "Zero-Base Budgeting," in Cheek, *Zero Base Budgeting Comes of Age*, p. 303. Cheek himself makes a similar statement in his summary to chapter 7 on page 154.
110. *The Politics of the Budgetary Process*, second edition, p. 207.
111. From Jong S. Jun, "Management-by-Objectives In Government: Theory and Practice," *Sage Professional Papers in Administrative and Policy Studies*, Paper 03-030 (Beverly Hills, Ca.: Sage Publications, 1976).
112. From Aaron Wildavsky, "Policy Analysis Is What Information Systems Are Not," Working Paper No. 53, June 1976, Graduate School of Public Policy, University of California, Berkeley, page 21. Reprinted in "Zero-Base Budget Legislation," Hearings Before The Task Force On Budget Process of the Committee on the Budget, House of Representatives, 94th Congress, Second Session, see page 129.
113. Cowan, "Zero-Base Budgeting," p. 14.
114. Farney, "Birth Pains," p. 1.

Chapter 5

Conclusion

The purpose of zero-base budgeting is to help managers make better budgetary choices. These better choices are to be achieved by following a number of seemingly-rational procedures. But despite this worthy purpose and the reasonable-looking method, ZBB has had little impact where tried.

That ZBB was designed without adequate understanding of the problems of government budgeting accounts for this lack of success. The rhetoric of reformers to the contrary, budgeters are not always inattentive to policy objectives and evaluation. More commonly, they lack the knowledge to design better policies; when the knowledge is available, they often lack the needed resources; and when the resources are available, they often lack the political support to implement their decisions. Just as well-meaning government programs are sometimes ill-adapted to the problems they are supposed to solve, so zero-base budgeting is ill-adapted to cope with these problems of government budgeting.

Modes of Rationality in Budgeting Reform

Like its predecessors—performance budgeting, PPBS, and Management by Objectives—zero-base budgeting rests upon a model of rationality that has a powerful logical and aesthetic appeal. Consider its well-known properties:

1. List all values relevant to the problem under consideration.
2. Specify carefully and precisely the objectives derived from these values.
3. Comprehensively list alternative ways of achieving the objectives.
4. Evaluate each alternative in terms of its ability to achieve the objectives.
5. Choose that alternative which maximizes achievement of the objectives.

As plausible and self-evident as these properties seem to be, each imposes conditions that government budgeters are seldom able to meet.

93

Steps one and two, listing values and specifying objectives, are supposed to make it easier to find out which values are most important, and what specific objectives should be pursued. But as we discussed in Chapter Two, specifying and clarifying values and objectives in government is a *political* process. Different goals have different supporters, and the supporters of each particular goal feel as they do with varying degrees of intensity. The key to a program's passage under these circumstances may be to leave objectives ambiguous. The managers of the resulting program are then in a position where they, and not the statute, can define the program's goals. But when Congress and the President are disinclined to specify goals clearly, program managers may avoid clarification for the same political reasons. Any goals which the program managers do develop under these conditions will undoubtedly come to include a measure of self-preservation not mentioned in the original statutes.

These first two steps also presume that in creating programs it is easy to know what our objectives are. This is less often the case than we realize. Goals are not just plucked out of the air. To a great extent they are the product of experience; we often don't know if we really want something until we actually try it. And given that sometimes we do know in advance what we like, *how much* we want of it is a function of the resources we have to spend on it, as we found in Chapter Three.

Step three, the comprehensive listing of alternative ways of achieving the objectives, appears unobjectionable. Having more options to choose among seems preferable to having fewer. But it may well be that most alternatives to current ways of doing things are politically or economically infeasible: there is neither enough support for them nor enough resources to implement them. We would particularly expect this to be the case when political and economic conditions are relatively stable and unchanging: all resources will be committed. To be sure, the times are occasionally so fluid and unsettled that large departures from the status quo are feasible. If such departures are indeed desirable, there is no reason why budgeters shouldn't take advantage of the opportunity and broaden their search for alternatives. But these favorable circumstances don't arise every year for every program; routinely compiling lists of alternatives may thus be a wasteful process.

More importantly, the assumption is implicitly made that alternatives are separate from objectives, that means are separate from ends. But ends may imply certain kinds of means, and a variety of alternatives may be incompatible with some kinds of objectives. Some of our most deeply-held values, for example, involve what we regard as "fair" or "democratic" procedures; other ways of doing things are simply ruled out of consideration, even though they may appear to be the most "efficient" way of achieving the objectives. Deciding which alternatives to consider is thus more complex than normally acknowledged. As often as the ends determine the means, the means available determine the ends.

Step four, evaluating the alternatives, is also problematic. The outputs of many government programs are not easily measured; recall the problems with performance measures discussed in Chapter Three. Evaluating hypothetical alternatives to these already hard-to-measure programs is many times more difficult. If in addition budgeters can't even agree on the goals of actual programs (steps one and two), or can't find alternatives satisfying disparate goals, their ability to evaluate alternatives to the programs suffers even more.[1]

Some program outputs can in principle be measured, but the public may not wish to find out exactly what the outputs are. Programs whose major purpose is to *prevent* something from happening are examples. Deterrence of nuclear attack by the Soviet Union is a major objective of American military policy. But if such an attack does not occur, we cannot be sure that our "deterrence" is the cause; the Soviet Union may simply have no desire to launch an attack. Similarly with crime prevention, we cannot be sure that the absence of burglaries in a neighborhood is a result of the police department's efforts or that there are simply no people who wish to commit crimes there. The best way to evaluate these programs is to suspend them, but we normally dare not do without nuclear deterrence and the local police, even for a short time.

Step five, making the final choice among alternatives, depends to a considerable degree on the successful completion of all the preceding steps. This is an unlikely occurrence. But assuming that these preceding steps have been carried out, the comparisons and calculations required for us to "maximize" achievement of our objectives may still be too complex for us to make. Even if we have an idea of the relevant values and objectives, and even if we have been able to specify and evaluate alternatives, there exists no agreed-upon calculus which tells us how to weigh one set of objectives against another. How do we integrate equity and efficiency into one single measure on which to base our decision? Talk of "maximization" in this context smacks more of bravado than of rationality.

It is often assumed, moreover, that the wise use of resources demands more than just the "local" maximization of a specific set of objectives. A comprehensive comparison of different objectives and alternatives is also implied: expenditures on national defense are, for example, to be compared with those on social welfare. But the more conscientiously we evaluate competing possible uses of scarce resources, the heavier the demands made on us, and the more our analysis is likely to bog down. This "global" maximization makes "local" maximization look easy.

Induction As a Mode of Rationality

For some kinds of governmental problems, the budget reformers' version of rationality may be useful: sometimes goals can be specified; sometimes the outputs of alternative programs can be objectively measured; sometimes it makes sense to speak of "maximization." But many problems are not amenable to this approach. They are "ill-structured" problems[2] in which "goals (and therefore 'success' and 'failure') are ambiguous or in conflict, in which what happened is unclear, and in which the causality of events is difficult to untangle."[3] The kind of rationality under consideration, however, is adapted only to "well-structured" problems.

We need not abandon rationality as a concern in decision making, however. We do need to realize, though, that the rationality under consideration is, at heart, a *deductive* rationality. Given a specific objective, a closed set of alternatives, complete information regarding their consequences, and criteria for choosing among them, choice becomes equivalent to a deductive process; the premises, in a logical sense, imply the conclusions. So appealing are the aesthetic simplicity and apparent universality of deductive rationality that it has become *synonymous* with rationality; no other way of solving problems is recognized. Yet budgeters are both too dumb and too smart to approach "ill-structured" problems in this way: too dumb because they usually cannot do what is called for; too smart because they use another mode of thought more appropriate for the circumstances. If the first kind of rationality is in essence a deductive rationality, this second kind is an *inductive* rationality.

Inductive rationality is a pattern-finding rationality; it is reasoning by analogy and metaphor. It is the rationality of "making sense" out of conflicting and ambiguous stimuli. Somehow from the welter of incoming data, we pick out those few "bits" which seem to "mean something" to us; all else is, for the moment at least, "noise." We have all had, for example, the "Aha!" experience, as in "Eureka! I just realized that *this* causes *that* to happen . . . I hadn't noticed it before!" When such patterns are discovered, certain decisions or actions seem to follow as a matter of course; the patterns themselves imply actions.

How do we draw these implications? Two separate processes appear to be involved: one is the recognition of context; the other is the accumulation of experience. The most common way we try to understand the context of a problem is to examine its history. When we try to figure out how to cope with a problem today, we almost invariably want to know whether we have seen the problem before; if we have, we want to recall what circumstances were like back then. If the problem seems to be unique, we make extensive searches of our memories for analogous events which can help us organize data about the current problem.[4] If such an analogy is found, we ask how our problem, or its analogue, was dealt with in the past: What did the decision makers do? How well did their "solutions" work? Then we speculate as to whether we should take the same actions, or whether we should do things differently: Can we improve upon their actions? If we do things differently, are we going to risk making things worse, and not better? Due to imperfect analogies and to other inevitable uncertainties, our decisions may well resemble those in the past only to a modest degree; we then let experience tell us whether we've done the right thing.

Inductive rationality as a mode of decision making in no way frees us from error. Errors are inevitable: analogies will break down; metaphors will become inappropriate; our understanding will fail us.[5] Given the provisional character of inductive thought, however, we are left relatively open to the perception of error so that we can correct it when it occurs.[6] Since neither excessive time nor much energy are normally invested in the discovery of such patterns, as compared with costs sunk in creating elaborate deductive systems, the patterns can be jettisoned more easily when action based on them fails. A search for more useful analogies or metaphors is then called for.[7]

As should be apparent, specifying the "rules" for induction is more difficult than for deduction. The process is not well understood. Those psychologists and computer scientists who have tried to write programs which draw deductions from premises have found them to be relatively easily written;[8] writing programs which can recognize patterns in complex data has proven immensely more difficult.[9] Yet pattern recognition is something that people do with relative ease. It is something that comes naturally to us; we may scarcely notice it while we are doing it.[10] Some kinds of pattern-recognition are, to be sure, more difficult than others. Though we recognize each other's faces with ease, learning a new language or an academic discipline is time-consuming. But the learning itself occurs at least in part through pattern recognition, and once "fluency" in the language is gained, whether in German or political science, recognition and incorporation of novel patterns into one's thought becomes almost second nature.

Drawing distinctions between induction and deduction would be beside the point if we were concerned about the accumulation of *scientific* knowledge; both processes are required in this case. The initial stages of scientific investigation—the recognition and definition of a problem, the development of hypotheses, and the choice of methods of investigation—all occur in an inductive mode; pattern recognition and the use of analogies and metaphors are as central to scientific creativity as they are to artistic expression. But scientists must ultimately adopt deductive modes of thought—hypothesis testing and the like—to determine if the pattern recognized is a "true" one.[11]

In public affairs, we would also like to have the time and resources to find out if what we merely suspect is really true.[12] But we are not usually afforded such a luxury: decisions have to be made next week and not next year, circumstances may change, we can't easily run experiments on people when their welfare and dignity are involved. So while governmental decision making may indeed suffer from the arrested development of which it is often accused, we nevertheless cannot leapfrog the inductive stage and proceed with the deductive activities involved in the second stage. In consequence, it seems ironic to us that when we are told to "be more rational," we are usually being told to do things we can't do at all well, instead of being urged to improve upon what we know we can do.

Since budgeters can't very often use the deductive-style procedures favored by budget reformers, the implication is that reformers should work at improving the inductive aspects of decision making. (We make a few suggestions along these lines later in the chapter.) Meanwhile, pending greater understanding of the inductive process, it is fortunate that ZBB's deductive-style procedures have proven so malleable in the hands of experienced budgeters; incremental budgeting is, after all, a form of inductive rationality.

Incremental Zero-Base Budgeting

Budgeters' annual need to settle allocations and the impossible-to-follow deductive character of ZBB's procedures conspired to maintain budgeting as it had been. When combined with the malleability of the procedures, the victory of incrementalism was complete: in no place did ZBB perform the way it was supposed to; in no instance did it bring about any significant changes, much less recognizable improvements, in resource allocation.

Managers used the same decision techniques as before. They did not want to reject the past, as the name "zero-base" budgeting implies;[13] instead, they explicitly wanted to take it into account as they made decisions. If nothing else, looking at what the agency did last year, its mistakes and failures as well as its successes, provided the readiest yardstick against which to measure new policies and programs. If they couldn't have looked at the past, they would have had to rely on theory to tell them what to do. Since available theories, especially in the social sciences, are not very good, they would have been left without any source of knowledge on which to base their decisions. Ignoring the past also would have been politically hazardous. Budgets create stable expectations among participants, both in the government and out, about what their share of scarce resources is going to be. Upsetting these expectations is costly. So budgeters felt it essential to build upon choices and agreements already established.

The decision packages were to be the building blocks of Pyhrr's system, with their minimums, performance measures, and alternatives. But budgeters found themselves relying to a considerable degree on the historical data in the packages. Budget negotiations within the agencies and with the central budget offices came to be premised on these historical comparisons. In New Mexico, for example, current allocations became the minimums in much the same way they become the "base" in traditional budgeting. In most other cases, an arbitrary figure of some eighty to ninety percent of the current budget came to be the minimum, and together with the next incremental package or two, which brought the total close to one hundred percent, they became the base for funding requests.

Further emphasizing this orientation around the historical base was the widespread use of expenditure guidelines. The guidelines focused program managers' attention on the decision packages proposing marginal changes from current expenditures. These guidelines are often used in traditional budgeting to keep expenditure requests from being too unrealistic (that is, too much higher than current levels), and under ZBB they had the added virtue of keeping the "income effect" from totally disabling the ranking process. Investigation of how the guidelines themselves were set would undoubtedly show a strong historical component.

The performance measures compiled for the decision packages could be interpreted for the most part only through historical comparisons. Budgeters in the Consumer Product Safety Commission, for example, complained that insufficient historical cost data existed. The fact of rising or falling costs told them little about what they should be doing;

some sort of context was needed. Inter-agency comparisons may have been possible, but with different agencies having different missions, comparing costs was difficult. The drawing of historical comparisons within the agencies commonly proved to be the preferred way of interpreting these data.

Middle- and upper-level budgeters initially found ranking the decision packages to be an exasperating process, due to the lack of common standards of comparison, to the interdependence of packages, and to the income effect. But the problem was greatly simplified when they realized that what really mattered was how packages were ranked around the probable cutoff line; the context for their decisions was thus set by these expectations. The ranking of packages lying above and below this zone was thus irrelevant: packages above the zone were going to be funded anyway, and packages below the zone weren't going to be funded, whatever their ranking. Even these rankings around the cutoff line, though they were ostensibly comparisons of future spending alternatives by different agencies, were probably heavily influenced by historical comparisons. Past experience with the uses to which previous increases were put—"Did they use last year's increases wisely?"—may have affected inclinations to award further increases for the upcoming year.

The decision techniques of most use to budgeters—the making of historical comparisons and the setting of contexts—were for the most part not augmented by ZBB. Only one of its procedures seems to have any potential for aiding decision making: this is the packaging of spending proposals around the margin. Despite the contradiction in terms, it is not unreasonable to wonder whether this aspect of *zero-base* budgeting might actually improve *incremental* budgeting.

Is ZBB a Better Incrementalism?

Has ZBB made a contribution to budgeting through its neat and tidy packaging of marginal spending proposals? In reducing an infinite number of possible marginal changes to a simpler, more comprehensible list of options, decision makers' choices may be clarified and simplified, and thereby improved. Some budgeters think that this is ZBB's major contribution. As the then-director of management and finance of the Department of Agriculture commented in 1978 after a year's experience with ZBB, "When you're through with zero-base budgeting, you have the best incremental budgeting system I've ever seen."[14]

The budgeter from Health, Education, and Welfare who commented that ". . . ZBB focused more attention upon marginal changes, up and down, than in the past'' (we cited this in Chapter 4) concluded that the ''chief advantage'' of ZBB was the fact that

> [I]t provides top level executives with building blocks of various sizes and shapes so that they can take some from here and add there and thereby make needed renovations in the budget house, albeit probably more minor ones than major ones. But it would be naive to assume otherwise. [15]

In a discussion of the incremental aspects of ZBB, Draper and Pitsvada point out that other budgeters also liked the formal and systematic display of options: the specific options didn't have to be formulated at the top levels; they were ready-made. [16]

Ranking packages around the margin, or at least grouping them in categories of importance around the margin (as was done in the Department of Defense), does seem potentially useful. Top decision makers don't always have time to formulate their own options; if a reasonable set of options can be provided, the decision makers may be better off. Providing such options is remarkably similar, moreover, to what Merewitz and Sosnick recommend when they criticize the ''zero-base'' aspects of PPBS. [17]

With the provision of these ''building blocks'' we have no quarrel. They are aids to calculation; their utility lies in the fact that they help the budgeter home in on an allocation of resources that seems reasonable to him. But it is not clear how innovative this is; it seems to us quite similar to other ''packaging'' techniques already in frequent use. Allocating money in ''round numbers'' to various agencies, for example, is another such packaging technique, and the content of any decision package has, in truth, little more theoretical significance. Budgeters themselves seem to recognize that the packages should not be treated as sacrosanct, since they are sometimes inclined to split open the last remaining unranked packages close to the cutoff line and distribute this money among a wide variety of activities. Although Draper and Pitsvada criticize this practice as contrary to ZBB tenets, [18] there is in fact no theoretical reason whatsoever (not even in the ZBB literature) that says these incremental decision packages should be of a certain size.

If pre-packaging is neither novel nor sacrosanct, how about the practice of arranging the packages around the margin? Is this an improvement over *current* practice? Apparently not, for one commentator on ZBB in the federal government refers to ''the age-old practice of internally (within the agency) budgeting for percentage decreases (just

in case) . . ."[19] More specifically, one Defense Department budgeter
noted, in his discussion of ZBB in DOD, that during the Eisenhower
years, "Typically each department head would be asked to justify not
only that budget level [their budget request], but also what he would
delete if the budget were 5-10% lower, and what he would add, if it
were 5-10% higher than that."[20] These calculations, while broader in
scope than decision packages are supposed to be, are nonetheless similar in principle. Even the arranging of options around the margin, it
appears, occurs already, if only in an informal way.

So while these aspects of zero-base budgeting may be valuable, they
are barely unique. And if they are the only remaining virtue of ZBB,
look how far we have departed from the original, "pure" ZBB: we
have abandoned objective specification, performance measurement,
consideration of alternatives, minimum package construction, and the
ranking of packages; only a few decision packages around the margin
need be created, and these need not be ranked to be useful for decisions. At this point we are inclined to agree with Robert Anthony of
the Harvard Business School when he remarks about ZBB that "the
new parts are not good, and the good parts are not new."[21]

Is ZBB a better form of incrementalism? At this point, we think the
distinction has become trivial: ZBB has so metamorphosed into incremental budgeting that the only thing left is its smile floating in the air.

If ZBB Doesn't Work, Why Is It Being Implemented?

It is ironic that managers who adopt ZBB demand less justification
for it than they do for the governmental programs which ZBB is to
help them scrutinize. There is no evidence from state and local government that ZBB has lived up to expectations, and yet we find it being
implemented on a large scale in the federal government. What can
account for this discrepancy? Some of the reasons which explain why
managers continue to like ZBB even after using it for a while, as we
have described in Chapter 4, probably help explain why it is adopted
in the first place.

It is undeniably true that effecting an appearance of concern about
governmental inefficiency and ineffectiveness is an important electoral
strategy for would-be chief executives. Such posturing, whether cyni-
cal or not, is a time-honored political practice; election and re-election
are felt to be difficult without it. Even after the election, actual adoption
of impressive-looking administrative reforms may increase the legiti-
macy of the administration among the population.

Other motives for the adoption of management techniques are less symbolic and more substantive in character. These techniques may give the new administration a temporary advantage over the bureaucracy itself; civil servants will have to learn a new language and adopt new procedures which the newcomers know (or act like they know) better than the bureaucrats do. Thus, the rationalistic appearance of the reforms may give the new administration opportunity to accomplish changes that might otherwise not be possible.

Additional motives probably stem from the frustration of actually trying to improve policy outcomes. Since many of the difficulties in public administration lie outside the bureaucracy—recalcitrant interest groups, intractable congressional committees, an indifferent public— the apparently unavoidable urge of managers is to turn in desperation to those facets of government which they feel they *can* control, that is, the procedures by which decisions are made. This kind of "displacement activity" (as animal behaviorists would call it) is of limited utility to the decision makers if the most easily-changed procedures have little to do with program outcomes, as we suspect is often the case.

Aiding and abetting the adoption of administrative reforms is the fact that those who decree their adoption—the top political executives— are seldom the ones who have to bear the costs of implementation and possible failure. What political benefits there are for these executives materialize quickly, since the benefits are often of a mostly-symbolic character. The costs, such as time, effort, and ultimate frustration, affect others much later. Finding out if one's budget reforms have actually produced greater efficiency and effectiveness is a time-consuming and difficult process. When the results are ambiguous or negative, and the costs do come back to haunt the top executives, we often find that these people have moved on to other jobs in the administration or have left government entirely. Those who remain—the career civil servants who have lived through PPBS and MBO and now ZBB—are the ones who have borne the costs and accumulated the experience, but they are seldom consulted about such matters. So due to the rapid turnover among the political appointees at the top of the government, and due to the difficulty of understanding what the effects of the reforms actually are, it may be that no substantive learning actually takes place. Even such useful knowledge about what *doesn't* work may be lost.

While these short-run benefits may motivate the adoption of management and budgeting "reforms," the long-run costs (which were discussed in detail inChapter 4) may be of greater consequence. If the reforms do not work well and are expensive to implement, the government runs less efficiently with the reforms than without: paperwork, specialized personnel, and operational disruption all increase, while output remains static or declines. Skepticism and cynicism may spread both in the affected agencies and among the public at large.

The prestige and influence of the federal government may also induce the spread of these effective-sounding but unproductive procedures. PPBS, MBO, and now ZBB are cases in point. Rather than employing the new procedures as political strategies to gain time and support for other worthwhile programs, state and local governments adopt them mostly because it is the fashionable thing to do. But without the short-term political utility, only the long-term policy-making costs remain. As a result, what benefits there may be are concentrated in one place— Washington D.C.—while the costs are exported almost everywhere else.

Are There Ways Of Getting The Benefits Of Budgeting Reforms Without All The Costs?

Inventing procedures which actually improve policy-making is not very easy. It may be harder to think about the rationality of decision procedures than it is to think about the rationality of substantive government programs themselves. The difficulties of writing a constitution—procedures which govern the activities of a national government—testify to this point. The reform of budget procedures, while certainly not as broad in scope as constitution-writing, seems to be equally complex, if one judges from the checkered history of budget reform.

As should be apparent by now, budgeting can have several incompatible purposes. People's goals and interests vary, as do their desires for various kinds of information. What the lower-level program director needs to know is different from what his agency's head requires for decision making; what the program director is willing to tell others may be incompatible with what upper management wants to find out. Allen Schick, for example, once pointed out that a budget that is useful for controlling how funds are spent is not one that is useful for management, and one that is useful for management is not useful for planning. He went on to warn us that, "As a practical matter, these three functions are competitive; emphasis on one diminishes use of the others."[22]

ZBB was originally motivated by a desire to instill more evaluation and justification in the budgetary process; allocation, it was felt, had come to dominate budgeting. These particular purposes are certainly somewhat incompatible, and concern has even been expressed that if evaluation and justification become the major concerns of budgeting, allocation will be neglected. LaFaver comments, for example, that:

> A budget addressed to justifying an agency's existence does not examine the critical issue facing a finance committee—that of how much should be allocated. Particularly in the large agencies, there is no real question but that the agencies will continue to operate. The question is, "At what level?"[23]

Like the ZBB proponents, however, we don't think it likely that allocation will come to be neglected. As in all forms of decision making, that which needs to be done today (such as allocation) tends to drive out that which can be done tomorrow (such as the overall evaluation of a program). To marry to zero-base budgeting (or to any other kind of budgeting, for that matter) anything more far-reaching than evaluation of proposals at the margin may simply mean that this kind of evaluation continues to be neglected. There is scant evidence from the ZBB cases, for example, that any serious evaluation in fact took place. In one sad case, concern with following ZBB procedures in routine allocation matters actually subverted a more fundamental piece of policy evaluation that had been done independently of ZBB procedures. This occurred during the congressional hearings of NASA's ZBB experiment. (See our discussion in Chapter 4). The House Appropriations Subcommittee members spent many hours quizzing NASA on its fidelity to ZBB procedures, while almost completely ignoring (to NASA's undoubted relief) the critical report that congressional staffers had prepared on NASA's Space Shuttle program.

Even Peter Pyhrr expresses some ambivalence about ZBB's ability to accomplish this kind of evaluation through the budgetary process. At one point he comments that since managers at all organizational levels have the same information, as provided in the decision packages and rankings, and since the top-level people have assured themselves that the proper analyses have been done, they can concentrate their activities more on establishing priorities "and less on their own independent fact finding and analysis."[24] But later he also observes that zero-base budgeting "in many cases . . . only scratches the surface of a problem area or indicates that a problem may exist." When this is the case, management "must then employ its analytic resources to investigate in detail and resolve the problem . . ." through investigation or an "operational audit."[25]

Pyhrr's caution is commendable. Yet the belief that ZBB makes "independent fact-finding and analysis" less necessary appears to predominate among those who adopt ZBB in government. Otherwise, what would have been the rationale for adopting such comprehensive procedures in the first place? The danger, of course, is that allocation will then continue to drive out evaluation.

This is not to deny that there are problems in getting adequate amounts of good evaluation in government budgeting. The question is how to get it, and make sure that it can be used. Since we can expect that inductive decision making techniques will continue to be the most appropriate for government budgeting, what we need are procedures that will help budgeters and managers understand a problem's context and accumulate useful experiences.

How can budgeters and managers come to understand what agencies are doing, especially when poor performance becomes a motivation for concealing or distorting information? Every organization has biases—preferred things to do and preferred ways of doing them—which stem from the skills, interests, and backgrounds of the members and from the external political demands made on the organization. Managerial and budgeting "reforms" generally either ignore the biases or attempt to eliminate them. Such efforts will invariably fail.[26]

The most common, and perhaps most important, way for top managers to cope with bias is to create a staff of analysts responsible only to themselves. This staff can devote itself to ferreting out information and creating options not produced by the bureaucracy. But there are limits to this strategy; many managers are not given authority to hire the required staff.

Another strategy to combat bias is to *rely* on the biases that organizations have in order to better inform decision makers. Multiple and competitive analysis by organizations of each other is better than singular analysis of oneself by oneself.[27] Does a proposed Corps of Engineers dam need evaluation? Don't rely just on the self-evaluation by the Corps and its "domesticated" in-house economic and ecological experts. Ask what the dam does to the interests of the Fish and Wildlife Service, the Forest Service, the Environmental Protection Agency, state fish and game departments, local businesses, and a host of other agencies and private interests. They are the ones who will be concerned enough to challenge the Corps' numbers.

How can we be sure that agencies will care about what each other do, so that we can rely on vigorously competitive evaluation to occur? People who adopt budget reforms often believe that, as part of the effort to make government more efficient, duplication and overlap among agencies should be eliminated; this is as hallowed a doctrine as there is in reform and reorganization circles. Yet it is only when there is some duplication of functions and overlap of jurisdictions that agencies will even care to contest each other's analyses and programs.[28] Just as there are virtues in competition among firms in a market, so there are virtues in some degree of competition among government agencies. Monopoly in government may be as unwise as in a market system.

How can managers accumulate useful experience? Surprisingly, the much-maligned line-item budget for an agency can play a useful role in informing decision makers. This kind of budget contains historical data useful for comparing past, current, and future actions. Line-item budgets are not, of course, the only budget formats which allow historical comparisons; historical comparisons of program outputs are certainly also possible. Over the long run, however, historical comparisons will be possible only if the program categories remain the same over time. This will most likely happen when the categories have some concrete or conceptually distinct character which is not readily changed or manipulated. But few program categories are this distinct; they seem, rather, to be extraordinarily flexible, as Nienaber and Wildavsky showed with respect to the Forest Service and Park Service under PPBS in the 1960s.[29] Agency boundaries are in contrast more likely to remain the same over time, and hence comparability can be maintained. Line-item budgets may not have all the whistles and bells of the more sophisticated formats, but they do have the virtue that people can easily agree on just what a budget entry means, and how it can be compared with the past and the future.

Generating information is a waste of time if those for whom it is generated can't use it. Some managerial and budgeting reforms may hinder managers' ability to absorb information, and thereby accumulate useful experience. PPBS generated so much paperwork—Program Review Memoranda and the like—that top managers could not cope with it. For its own part, ZBB produces vast numbers of decision packages to be ranked by top managers; if top managers actually ranked all the packages they are supposed to, they would be left with little time for a more searching analysis of any one program.

The scarcest resource of all in government budgeting is not money so much as the time and energy of top decision makers. What they need are not aids to comprehensiveness but aids to selectivity: they need to know which problem it makes the most sense to work on, of all those meriting attention. The history of a problem and its current political context may be the best guides. When the problem is "ripe" for solution, when an alternative is available and the political support for it can be assembled, the top manager can invest his time wisely. If these preconditions do not exist, attention to other issues may be the better part of wisdom.

Another context-setting aid to selectivity is the focusing of attention on marginal changes to existing programs. Instead of trying to evaluate whole programs when doing so won't change things, decision makers can make judgments about where any *changes* in program allocations should take place. This is where the packaging of options around the margin may be helpful. While it may be impossible to revise an ineffective but popular program, it may be feasible to deny it further increases or even whittle it down a bit. Money then saved could be spent elsewhere, or not spent at all.

If government managers followed our advice, budgeting in government would still look rather like what we have right now; it would certainly not resemble the model of rationality embodied by ZBB. It would, however, have a peculiar saving grace: it would work. Zerobase budgeting doesn't.

Notes

1. In *Evaluation and Reform: The Elementary and Secondary Education Act of 1965, Title I* (Cambridge, Mass.: Ballinger, 1975), Milbrey Wallin McLaughlin recounts the difficulties experienced in evaluating this particular educational program. One of the greatest problems was that the program's strongest supporters disagreed on what the purpose of the program actually was.
2. A term, along with its counterpart, "well-structured" problems, used by Allen Newell in "Heuristic Programming: Ill-Structured Problems" in Julius S. Aronofsky (editor), *Progress in Operations Research*, Vol. III, Publications in Operations Research, No. 16, Operations Research Society of America (New York: John Wiley & Sons, 1969), p. 363.
3. A description by James G. March and Johan P. Olsen in their "The Uncertainty of the Past: Organizational Learning Under Uncertainty," *European Journal of Political Research* 3 (June 1975), p. 148.
4. Regarding legal reasoning, Edward H. Levi comments, "The basic pattern . . . is reasoning by example. It is reasoning from case to case. . . . [T]he scope of a rule of law, and therefore its meaning, depends upon a determination of what facts will be considered similar to those present when the rule was first announced. The finding of similarity or difference is the key step in the legal process." From *An Introduction To Legal Reasoning* (Chicago, Ill.: University of Chicago Press, 1949), pp. 1, 2. This kind of process is considered in detail in Robert Axelrod's "Schema Theory: An Information Processing Model of Perception and Cognition," *American Political Science Review* 67 (December 1973).
5. March and Olsen, in their "The Uncertainty of the Past: Organizational Learning Under Uncertainty," discuss a number of ways in which organizational learning of this sort can break down.

6. This is not to say that people don't on occasion take their analogies and metaphors as "facts." For a discussion of this problem, see Ernest R. May, *"Lessons" of the Past: The Use and Misuse of History in American Foreign Policy* (New York: Oxford University Press, 1973).

7. Similar kinds of problem-motivated search are described by Richard M. Cyert and James G. March in *A Behavioral Theory of the Firm* (Englewood Cliffs, N.J.: Prentice-Hall, 1963), and by Robert Axelrod in "Schema Theory."

8. At the simplest level are most programming languages like FORTRAN which can draw deductions of the "if . . . then" type. Some of the most ambitious efforts at writing deductive, theorem-proving programs have been made by Allen Newell and Herbert Simon. See their *Human Problem Solving* (Englewood Cliffs, N.J.: Prentice-Hall, 1972).

9. Statistical curve-fitting routines (such as the drawing of regression lines) whose mathematics looks complex are in fact quite simple in conception. The human hand and eye can do reasonably accurately what these routines do.

10. Sometimes we can become so adept at finding patterns that we see them even where there are none. Paranoia is an illness of this sort.

11. Abraham Kaplan distinguishes between what he calls "the pattern model" of explanation and the "deductive model" in his *The Conduct of Scientific Inquiry* (San Francisco, Ca.: Chandler Publishing Company, 1964). As he explains, "Very roughly, we know the reason for something either when we can fit it into a known pattern, or else when we can deduce it from other known truths." He also comments that, "The pattern model may more easily fit explanations in early stages of inquiry, and the deductive model explanations in later stages." (pp. 332ff).

   It should be noted, however, that to Kaplan both the pattern model and the deductive model are examples of what he calls "reconstructed logic": what the logic *would* be "if it were extracted and refined to utmost purity." (p. 11). The "cognitive style" that scientists actually use in their investigations he calls "logic-in-use." (p. 8). Given that induction as it is described here is inadequately specified (because we do not understand it very well), we cannot quarrel with calling our description a "reconstructed logic."

12. In a sense, any patterns which have been discerned and any plans and programs based on them may be seen as hypotheses which ideally would be tested in a scientific manner. Martin Landau stresses this point in his essay, "On the Concept of a Self-Correcting Organization," *Public Administration Review* 33 (November/December 1973).

13. In 1977 Pyhrr stressed that the term "zero-base" does not mean "the process of throwing everything out and starting all over again from scratch" or "reinventing the wheel." But then he goes on to say that "In a more practical vein, 'zero-base' means the evaluation of *all* programs." (Emphasis added). Practically speaking, this strikes us as a distinction without a difference. See Peter Pyhrr, "The Zero-Base Approach To Government Budgeting," *Public Administration Review* 37 (January/February 1977), p. 7.

14. Jerome A. Miles, quoted in Joel Havemann, "The Budget—A Tax Cut, Little Else," *National Journal* 10 (28 January 1978), p. 129.

15. Thomas W. De Hanas, "Zero-base Budgeting and the Management Review Process in the Department of Health, Education and Welfare," *The Bureaucrat* 7 (Spring 1978), p. 25.
16. Frank D. Draper and Bernard Pitsvada, *A First Year Assessment*, pp. 58-59.
17. See Leonard Merewitz and Stephen H. Sosnick, *The Budget's New Clothes: A Critique of Planning-Programming-Budgeting and Benefit-Cost Analysis* (Chicago, Ill.: Markham, 1971), chapter 5, "Zero-Base Budgeting." In his *Zero-Base Budgeting and Program Evaluation* (Lexington, Mass.: Lexington Books, 1978), Joseph Wholey proposes a "simplified" version of ZBB which is much the same: the creation of decision packages for comparison around an expenditure guideline.
18. *A First Year Assessment*, p. 49.
19. See Richard Miller, "ZBB in the Federal Government," p. 8.
20. John R. Quetsch, "ZBB and DoD," *The Bureaucrat* 7 (Spring 1978), p. 33.
21. "Zero-Base Budgeting: A Useful Fraud?" *The Government Accountants Journal* 26 (Summer 1977), p. 9.
22. *Budget Innovation in the States*, p. 4.
23. John D. LaFaver, "Zero-Base Budgeting in New Mexico," *State Government* 27 (Spring 1974), p. 109.
24. Pyhrr, *Zero-Base Budgeting*, p. 33.
25. Ibid, p. 184.
26. If one needs further convincing of this, consult Aaron Wildavsky's entertaining tale of "Evaluation, Incorporated" in his "The Self-Evaluating Organization," *Public Administration Review* 32 (September/October 1972).
27. Using competitive analysis to generate useful information may heighten the conflicts implicit in the budgetary process. But unlike the conflicts fostered by ZBB through requirements for clarification of objectives, and so forth, which may simply make bureaucrats fight more, competitive analysis fosters conflicts which produce politically important information for decision makers.
28. For a well-developed theoretical elaboration of this general point, see Martin Landau's "Redundancy, Rationality, and the Problem of Duplication and Overlap," *Public Administration Review* 29 (July/August 1969).
29. *The Budgeting and Evaluation of Federal Recreation Programs*, chapter 5.

Appendix

Why Incremental Decision Packages
May Often Be Unrankable

Let us assume (1) that managers in organizations behave in the completely rational manner intended by ZBB proponents, (2) that we can directly measure and thus compare the outputs (benefits) of different programs, and (3) that we know the production functions of the different programs, that is, we know what outputs can be produced for every combination of inputs. (All three assumptions are of course questionable.) Imagine three particular programs and their associated production functions, shown in the following figure.

Now give the manager in charge of the three programs a small amount of money, m_1. How should he allocate it among the three programs? If he allocates it all to Program 1, he will produce O_1 in benefits. If he gives it entirely to Program 2, he will produce O_2 in benefits, which is less than O_1. And if he spends it entirely on Program 3, he does even worse, producing only O_3 in benefits. The rational decision is to allocate all of m_1 to Program 1: output O_1 is bigger than outputs O_2 and O_3.

If the manager receives more and more money and he continues to spend it on Program 1, the benefits produced by each additional dollar gradually decline. (Another way of saying this is that the marginal rate of production of benefits is decreasing. The marginal rate of production of benefits at point a_1 is equal to the slope of line A_1 where it is tangent to the production function curve at a_1.) When expenditures exceed m_2, however, the benefits produced by each additional dollar in Program 1 become so low that it makes sense to start allocating some of the money to Program 2. Not *all* the money in excess of m_2 should be spent on Program 2 though; this money should be allocated proportionally between the two programs so that the benefits gained from expenditure of each additional dollar on Program 2 between a_2 and b_2

111

Figure 1

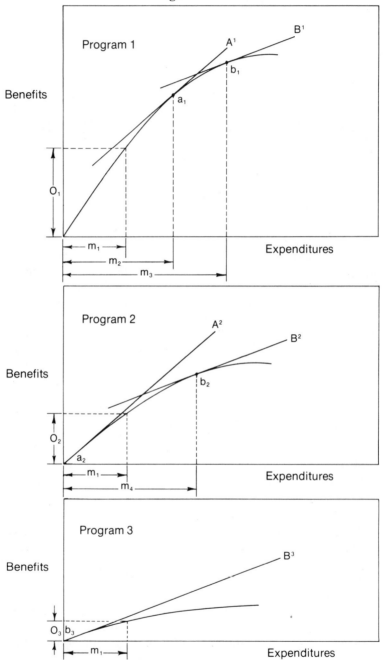

equal the benefits gained from each additional dollar spent on Program 1 between a_1 and b_1. Another way of saying this is that expenditures exceeding m_2 should be made in such a way that the ratio of marginal benefits to marginal costs for Program 2 is the same as the ratio of marginal benefits to marginal costs for Program 1. In a sense, then, the marginal benefits and costs of the two programs are (should be) equal.

Recall at this point that zero-base budgeting procedures require a manager to rank in order of priority not only his ongoing programs but also any increments in spending for these programs. These increases are referred to as incremental decision packages. But our analysis has just demonstrated that a given marginal (incremental) increase in expenditure for Programs 1 and 2 should be spent in such a way that *equal* benefits are produced by both programs. Decision packages based on these increments, therefore, would also be equal in importance and *could not be ranked*. The *total* benefits produced in Program 1 are higher than in Program 2, but the marginal benefits (i.e., the rate of production of benefits from each additional dollar), on which the incremental decision packages would be based, should be the same for a given increase in expenditures.

If the manager's budget is increased even further, ultimately the benefits produced by each additional dollar in both Programs 1 and 2 decrease so much that it becomes rational to start allocating some of the increased budget to Program 3. (The slopes of B_1 at b_1 for Program 1, of B_2 at b_2 for Program 2 and of B_3 at b_3 for Program 3 are all equal.) In this case when expenditures exceed m_3 (on Program 1) plus m_4 (on Program 2), the money in excess of m_3+m_4 should be allocated among all three programs so that the benefits gained from expenditure of each additional dollar on Program 3 equal *both* the benefits gained from Program 2 beyond b_2 *and* the benefits gained from Program 1 beyond b_1. That is, the marginal rates of production of benefits for all three programs should be kept equal for expenditures in excess of m_3+m_4, and as before, in this range of expenditure, incremental decision packages should be of equal importance.

So only in a way not evident in ZBB's procedures can programs be ranked. As our budget increases from zero, we first allocate money only to Program 1, and it would "rank" higher than the other two programs; indeed, it would be inefficient to allocate money to either of them. Soon, however, it does make sense to add money to Program 2 and the rational manager would do it in such a way that he could not rank these increments. Program 3, however, is left unfunded, and hence could be thought to rank low. But soon it too should have money allocated to it, and again this should be done in such a way that the increments would all be of equal importance.

Now it is clear that the assumptions on which this whole line of analysis is based don't usually hold true. We don't often know what the production functions of government agencies look like, we cannot count on the kind of rationality of managers that ZBB proponents hope for, and we seldom can so easily compare outputs or benefits. But there is an important lesson nonetheless: *if* the assumptions on which ZBB is premised *were* true, then ZBB's ranking and cutoff line procedures would not work very well.

Incidentally, the reason why we don't run into the "knapsack problem" here is because we are assuming, we think reasonably, that programs are generally "divisible." ZBB makes budgeters artificially convert divisible programs into "lumpy" ones and thereby lays ZBB open to the logical flaw discussed at the end of Chapter 3.

Biographical Notes

Thomas H. Hammond is an Assistant Professor of Political Science at Purdue University in West Lafayette, Indiana. He received his Ph.D. in Political Science from the University of California in 1979. The topic of his dissertation was bureaucratic politics and organizational environments. He is the author of "Another Look At The Role Of 'The Rules' In The 1972 Democratic Primaries," *Western Political Quarterly* (forthcoming, 1980).

Jack H. Knott is an Assistant Professor of Political Science at Michigan State University in East Lansing, Michigan. He received his M.A. from Johns Hopkins University in 1971 and his Ph.D. from the University of California, Berkeley in 1977. His dissertation, "Accommodating Purposes: Fiscal and Budgetary Policy in West Germany," has been published in the IIM Paper Series, International Institute of Management Science Center, West Berlin, 1978. His other publications include "Stabilization Policy, Grants-in-Aid and the Federal System in West Germany," in Wallace Oates, ed., *The Political Economy of Fiscal Federalism*, (Lexington, Mass.: D. C. Heath, 1977); and "Jimmy Carter's Theory of Governing," (co-author, Aaron Wildavsky) *The Wilson Quarterly* 1 (Winter 1977).

Bibliography

Government Publications

U.S. Congress, Congressional Budget Office. *An Experiment in Zero-Base Budget Analysis—Fiscal Year 1978*. Interagency Energy/Environment R&D Program Report, March 1977.

U.S. Congress, House. Committee on Appropriations. *Hearings Before the Subcommittee on Appropriations, Part 4: Consumer Product Safety Commission*. 95th Cong., 1st sess., March 16-17, 1977.

U.S. Congress, House. Committee on Appropriations. *Hearings Before the Subcommittee on Appropriations, Part 5: National Aeronautics and Space Administration*. 95th Cong., 1st sess., March 29-30, 1977.

U.S. Office of Management and Budget. Bulletin No. 77-9: "Zero-Base Budgeting." *The Federal Register*, April 19, 1977, pp. 22342-54.

U.S. Congress, Senate. Committee on Governmental Operations, Subcommittee on Intergovernmental Relations. *Compendium of Materials on Zero-Based Budgeting in the States*. Washington D.C.: U.S. Government Printing Office, 1977. (This *Compendium* contains extracts from several unpublished or otherwise inaccessible sources, several of which are listed below.)

Books and Articles

Anthony, Robert N. "Zero-Base Budgeting: A Useful Fraud?" *The Government Accountants Journal* 26 (Summer 1977): 7-10.

Arrow, Kenneth. *The Limits of Organization*. New York: W.W. Norton, 1974.

Austin, L. Allan. "Zero-Base Budgeting: Organizational Impact and Effects." *AMA Survey Report*. New York: American Management Association, 1977.

Axelrod, Robert. "Schema Theory: An Information Processing Model of Perception and Cognition." *American Political Science Review* 69 (December 1973): 1248-66.

Blandin, Nanette M. and Donahue, Arnold E. "ZBB: Not A Panacea, But A Definite Plus—An OMB Perspective." *The Bureaucrat* 7 (Spring 1978): 51-55.

Bledsoe, Ralph C. "What Top Managers Ought To Know About ZBB." *The Bureaucrat* 7 (Spring 1978): 56-59.

Bower, Joseph. *Managing The Resource Allocation Process: A Study of Corporate Planning and Investment*. Boston, Mass.: Harvard Business School, 1970.

Carter, Luther. "Toxic Substances: Five Year Struggle for Landmark Bill May Soon Be Over." *Science* 194 (1 October 1976): 40-42.

Carter, Jimmy. "Zero-Base Budgeting." Printed in Logan M. Cheek, *Zero-Base Budgeting Comes of Age*. New York: American Management Association, 1977.

Carter, Jimmy. *Why Not The Best?* Nashville, Tenn.: Broadman Press, 1975.

Carter, Jimmy. "Budget Message of the President." *Congressional Quarterly Weekly Report* 36 (28 January 1978): 232-234.

Cheek, Logan M. *Zero-Base Budgeting Comes of Age: What It Is And What It Takes To Make It Work*. New York: The American Management Association, 1977.

Conger, Bruce C. "Zero-base Budgeting at the Department of Housing and Urban Development." *The Bureaucrat* 7 (Spring 1978): 45-47.

Cowan, Edward. "Zero-Base Budgeting—It Made A Difference." *The New York Times*, 22 January 1978, Section 3, pp. 1, 14.

Cyert, Richard M. and March, James G. *A Behavioral Theory of the Firm*. Englewood Cliffs, N.J.: Prentice-Hall, 1963.

Davis, Otto A., Dempster, M.A.H. and Wildavsky, Aaron. "Towards A Predictive Theory of Government Expenditure: U.S. Domestic Appropriations." *British Journal of Political Science* 4 (October 1974): 419-52.

De Hanas, Thomas W. "Zero-base Budgeting and the Management Review Process in the Department of Health, Education, and Welfare." *The Bureaucrat* 7 (Spring 1978): 22-25.

Draper, F. Dale and Pitsvada, Bernard T. "Zero-Base Budgeting in the Federal Government; Some Preliminary Observations On The First Year's Effort." *The Government Accountants Journal* 27 (Spring 1978): 22-30.

Draper, F. Dale and Pitsvada, Bernard T. *A First Year Assessment of Zero-Base Budgeting in the Federal Government—Another View*. Arlington, Va.: Association of Government Accountants, 1978.

Driessnack, Hans H. "Zero-base Budgeting: Our First Year." *The Bureaucrat* 7 (Spring 1978): 36-40.

Drucker, Peter. "MBO—Tool Or Master?" *The Federal Accountant* 24 (September 1975): 23-29.

Drucker, Peter. "What Results Should You Expect? A User's Guide To MBO." *Public Administration Review*. 36 (January/February 1976): 12-19.

Eaton, William J. "Zero-Base Budgeting—Some Say It's Nothing." *San Francisco Sunday Examiner-Chronicle*, 15 January 1978, Section C, p. 13.

Eckert, William A. "Evaluating The Impact of Zero-Base Budgeting." Unpublished paper presented at the Annual Meeting of the Midwest Political Science Association, Chicago, Illinois, April 20-22, 1978.

Etzioni, Amitai. "Mixed-Scanning: A 'Third' Approach To Decision-Making." *Public Administration Review* 27 (December 1967): 385-92.

Farney, Dennis. "Birth Pains: Zero-Base Budgeting, A Pet Carter Project, Is Off To A Slow Start." *The Wall Street Journal*, 19 December 1977, pp. 1,22.

Farney, Dennis. "Budget: Neither Fish Nor Fowl." *The Wall Street Journal*, 24 January 1978, p. 14.

Fauntleroy, Lefford B., Jr. "Reflections on ZBB: A Congressional Test and the Executive Mandate." *The Bureaucrat* 7 (Spring 1978): 10-14.

Fenno, Richard F. *The Power of the Purse*. Boston, Mass.: Little, Brown, 1966.

Gaver, Donald P. and Thompson, Gerald L. *Programming and Probability Models in Operations Research*. Monterey, Cal.: Brooks/ Cole, 1973.

Gist, John R. "Mandatory Expenditures and the Defense Sector: The Theory of Budgetary Incrementalism," *Sage Professional Papers in American Politics*, Number 04-020. Beverly Hills, Ca.: Sage Publications, 1974.

Kaplan, Abraham. *The Conduct of Scientific Inquiry*. San Francisco: Chandler, 1964.

Granof, Michael H. and Kinzel, Dale A. "Zero-Based Budgeting: Modest Proposal For Reform." *The Federal Accountant* 23 (December 1974): 50-56.

Haider, Donald F. "Zero Base, Federal Style." *Public Administration Review* 37 (July/August 1977): 400-407.

Havemann, Joel. "OMB Begins Major Program to Identify and Attain Presidential Goals." *National Journal* 5 (2 June 1973): 783-793.

Havemann, Joel. "Taking Up the Tools to Tame the Bureaucracy: Zero-Base Budgeting." *National Journal* 9 (2 April 1977): 514-517.

Havemann, Joel. "The Budget—A Tax Cut, Little Else." *National Journal* 10 (28 January 1978): 124-132.

Havemann, Joel. "The Tale of How One Agency Used ZBB—And Lived to Tell About It." *National Journal* 10 (18 February 1978): 265-269.

Heclo, Hugh. "Political Executives and the Washington Bureaucracy." *Political Science Quarterly* 92 (Fall 1977): 395-424.

Heclo, Hugh. *A Government of Strangers*. Washington D.C.: Brookings, 1977.

Hirschleifer, Jack. *Investment, Interest and Capital*. Englewood, Cliffs, N.J.: Prentice-Hall, 1970.

Hitch, Charles and McKean, Roland. *The Economics of Defense in the Nuclear Age*. Cambridge, Mass.: Harvard University Press, 1961.

Hogan, Roy Lee. "Zero-Base Budgeting: A Rationalistic Attempt to Improve the Texas Budget System." M.A. thesis in Public Administration, University of Texas, Austin, 1975. (Chapters 5, 6 and 7 are reprinted in *Compendium* listed under Government Publications above, pp. 224-317. All page references are to this latter source.)

Itteilag, Tony. "FY 1979 ZBB Formulation in the Public Health Service." *The Bureaucrat* 7 (Spring 1978): 15-21.

Jun, Jong S. "Management By Objectives in Government: Theory and Practice." *Sage Professional Papers in Administrative and Policy Studies*, Number 03-030. (Beverly Hills, Ca.: Sage Publications, 1976).

Kolata, Gina Bari. "National Bureau of Standards: A Fall From Grace." *Science* 197 (2 September 1977): 968-970.

LaFaver, John D. "Zero-Base Budgeting in New Mexico." *State Government* 47 (Spring 1974): 108-112.

Landau, Martin. "Redundancy, Rationality, and the Problem of Duplication and Overlap." *Public Administration Review* 29 (July/August 1969): 345-358.

Landau, Martin. "On The Concept of a Self-Correcting Organization." *Public Administration Review* 33 (November-December 1973): 533-542.

Large, Arlen. "Applying Zero-Base Budgeting." *The Wall Street Journal*, 24 May 1977, p. 20.

Lauth, Thomas P. "Zero-Base Budgeting in Georgia State Government: Myth and Reality." *Public Administration Review* 38 (September/October 1978): 420-430.

Levi, Edward H. *An Introduction To Legal Reasoning*. Chicago, Ill.: University of Chicago Press, 1949.

Lewis, Verne. "Toward A Theory of Budgeting." *Public Administration Review* 12 (Winter 1952): 42-54.

Lindblom, Charles E. "The Science of 'Muddling Through.' " *Public Administration Review* 19 (Spring 1959): 79-88.

Lindblom, Charles E. and Braybrooke, David. *A Strategy of Decision*. New York: The Free Press of Glencoe, 1963.

Lindblom, Charles. "Limitations on Rationality: A Comment." In *Rational Decisions, Nomos*, Volume VII, edited by Carl J. Friedrich, pp. 224-228. New York: Atherton Press, 1964.

Lindblom, Charles E. *The Intelligence of Democracy*. New York: The Free Press of Glencoe, 1965.

March, James G. "The Business Firm As A Political Coalition." *Journal of Politics* 24 (November 1962): 662-678.

March, James G. and Simon, Herbert A. *Organizations*. New York: Wiley, 1958.

March, James G. and Olsen, Johan P. "The Uncertainty of the Past: Organizational Learning Under Uncertainty." *European Journal of Political Research* 3 (June 1975): 147-171.

Markham, Emerson. "Zero-base Budgeting in ACTION." *The Bureaucrat* 7 (Spring 1978): 48-50.

Marz, Roger. "Myth, Magic and Administrative Innovations." *Administration and Society* 10 (August 1978): 131-38.

May, Ernest R. *"Lessons" of the Past: The Use and Misuse of History in American Foreign Policy*. New York: Oxford University Press, 1973.

McLaughlin, Milbrey Wallin. *Evaluation and Reform: The Elementary and Secondary Education Act of 1965, Title I*. Cambridge, Mass.: Ballinger, 1975.

Merewitz, Leonard and Sosnick, Stephen H. *The Budget's New Clothes: A Critique of Planning-Programming-Budgeting and Benefit-Cost Analysis*. Chicago, Ill.: Markham, 1971.

Merton, Robert K. "Bureaucratic Structure and Personality." In *Reader in Bureaucracy*, edited by Robert K. Merton, Ailsa P. Gray, Barbara Hockey, and Hanan C. Selvin, pp. 361-371. Glencoe, Ill.: The Free Press of Glencoe, 1952.

Miller, Richard E. "ZBB in the Federal Government: Some Current Impressions." *The Bureaucrat* 7 (Spring 1978): 5-9.

Mills, Herbert T. "Zero-base Budgeting: The Initial Experience in SBA." *The Bureaucrat* (Spring 1978): 26-30.

Minmier, George S. *An Evaluation of the Zero-Based Budgeting System in Governmental Institutions*. Atlanta, Georgia: School of Business Administration, Georgia State University, 1975. (Chapters 5 and 6 are reprinted in the *Compendium* listed under Government Publications above, pp. 133-212.)

Minmier, George S. and Hermanson, Roger. "A Look At Zero-Based Budgeting: The Georgia Experience." *Atlantic Economic Review* 26 (July-August 1976): 5-12. Reprinted in *The Government Accountants Journal* 25 (Winter 1976-77): 1-11.

Nagle, Jim. "Zero-Base Budgeting." *The Bureaucrat* 6 (Spring 1977): 152-55.

Navasky, Victor. *Kennedy Justice*. New York: Atheneum, 1971.

Natchez, Peter B. and Bupp, Irvin C. "Policy and Priority in the Budgetary Process." *American Political Science Review* 67 (September 1973): 951-963.

Newell, Allen. "Heuristic Programming: Ill-Structured Problems." In *Progress In Operations Research*, Vol. III, edited by Julius S. Aronofsky, pp. 361-414. Publications in Operations Research, No. 16, Operations Research Society of America. New York: John Wiley & Sons, 1969.

Newell, Allen and Simon, Herbert. *Human Problem Solving*. Englewood Cliffs, N.J.: Prentice-Hall, 1972.

Nienaber, Jeanne and Wildavsky, Aaron. *The Budgeting and Evaluation of Federal Recreation Programs, or Money Doesn't Grow on Trees*. New York: Basic Books, 1973.

Pyhrr, Peter A. "Zero-Base Budgeting." *Harvard Business Review* 48 (November-December 1970): 111-121.

Pyhrr, Peter A. *Zero-Base Budgeting: A Practical Management Tool For Evaluating Expenses*. New York: John Wiley & Sons, 1973.

Pyhrr, Peter A. "The Zero-Base Approach to Government Budgeting." *Public Administration Review* 37 (January/February 1977): 1-8.

Quetsch, John R. "ZBB and DoD." *The Bureaucrat* 7 (Spring 1978): 31-35.

Roark, Anne C. "Whodunit? Intrigue? Mystery! False Clues!" *The Chronicle of Higher Education*, 6 February 1978, pp. 10-11.

Rourke, Francis. *Bureaucracy, Politics and Public Policy*, 1st ed. Boston, Mass.: Little, Brown, 1969.

Sanders, Ralph. *The Politics of Defense Analysis*. New York: Dunellen, 1973.

Sapolsky, Harvey. *The Polaris System Development*. Cambridge, Mass.: Harvard University Press, 1972.

Scheiring, Michael J. "Zero-Based Budgeting in New Jersey" in the *Compendium* listed under Government Publications above, pp. 363-384.

Schick, Allen. *Budget Innovation in the States*. Washington D.C.: The Brookings Institution, 1971.

Schick, Allen. "A Death in the Bureaucracy: The Demise of Federal PPB." *Public Administration Review* 33 (March/April 1973): 146-156.

Schick, Allen and Keith, Robert. "Zero Base Budgeting in the States," in the *Compendium* listed under Government Publications above, pp. 4-52.

Schick, Allen. "Statement on Zero-Base Budget Legislation." In Hearings Before the Task Force on Budget Processes of the Committee on the Budget, House of Representatives, 94th Cong., 2nd sess., June 30, July 27-28, 1976. Reprinted in *Zero-Base Budgeting Comes of Age* by Logan M. Cheek. New York: American Management Association, 1977.

Schick, Allen. "Zero-Base Budgeting and Sunset: Redundancy or Symbiosis?" *The Bureaucrat* 6 (Spring 1977): 12-32.

Schick, Allen. "The Road From ZBB." *Public Administration Review* 38 (March/April 1978): 177-180.

Simon, Herbert A. *Administrative Behavior*. New York: The Free Press, 1945.

Singleton, David W., Smith, Bruce A. and Cleaveland, James R. "Zero-Base Budgeting in Wilmington, Delaware." *The Bureaucrat* 6 (Spring 1977): 67-87.

Smith, R. Jeffrey. "Carter Budget Tilts 'Back to Basics' for Research: Environmental Protection Agency." *Science* 199 (3 February 1978): 509.

Stonich, Paul J. *Zero-Base Planning and Budgeting: Improved Cost Control and Resource Allocation*. Homewood, Ill.: Dow Jones-Irwin, 1977.

Suver, George and Brown, Ray. "Where Does Zero-Base Budgeting Work?" *Harvard Business Review* 55 (November-December 1977): 76-84.

Taylor, Serge. "Institutionalizing Analysis of Secondary Impacts in Government Agencies." Ph.D. dissertation, University of California, Berkeley, forthcoming.

Turnbull, Augustus B. "Politics in the Budgetary Process: The Case of Georgia." Ph.D. dissertation, University of Georgia, Athens, Georgia, 1967.

Wholey, Joseph. *Zero-Base Budgeting and Program Evaluation.* Lexington, Mass.: Lexington Books, 1978.

Wildavsky, Aaron. *The Politics of the Budgetary Process.* 2d ed. Boston, Mass.: Little, Brown, 1974.

Wildavsky, Aaron and Hammann, Arthur. "Comprehensive Versus Incremental Budgeting in the Department of Agriculture." *Administrative Science Quarterly* 10 (December 1965): 321-346.

Wildavsky, Aaron. "The Self-Evaluating Organization." *Public Administration Review* 32 (September/October 1972): 509-520.

Wildavsky, Aaron and Caiden, Naomi. *Planning and Budgeting in Poor Countries.* New York: John Wiley & Sons, 1974.

Wildavsky, Aaron. *Budgeting.* Boston, Mass.: Little, Brown, 1975.

Wildavsky, Aaron. "Policy Analysis Is What Management Information Systems Are Not." Working Paper No. 53. Berkeley, California: Graduate School of Public Policy, July 1976.

Wilensky, Harold. *Organizational Intelligence.* New York: Basic Books, 1967.

Wilson, James Q. "Zero-Base Budgeting Comes to Washington." *The Alternative: An American Skeptic*, February 1977, p. 5.

Witcover, Jules. *Marathon.* New York: The Viking Press, 1977.

Wooten, James T. "Carter's Campaign Is Producing A Broad Range Of Impressions." *The New York Times*, 11 February 1976, p. 26.

Wooten, James T. "Carter's Way With Issues Bothers Voters." *The New York Times*, 15 March 1976, p. 36.

Index

ACTION, 17, 45-48

Activities: categorization of, 14-17; evaluation of, 18; and minimum level of effort, 35-36; political costs and benefits of, 14. *See also* Objectives

Agriculture, U. S. Department of: benefits of ZBB for, 67-69; costs of ZBB for, 80-81; incremental budgeting in, 100; use of PPBS in, 15; ranking programs in, 45. *See also* Program budgeting

Air Force, U. S., 15, 75

Alternatives: choosing of, 33-34; evaluation of, 40-41, 105; listing of, 94-96; presentation of, 40. *See also* Comprehensive decision making

Anthony, Robert N., 102

Appropriations Subcommittee, U. S. House of Representatives—NASA, 82, 105

Army, U. S., 75

Army Corps of Engineers, U. S., 21, 106

Baucus, Max, Congressman, 38, 43-44, 70. *See also* Appropriations Subcommittee, U. S. House of Representatives—NASA

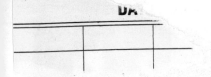